ENTERTAINMENT

by Linda Peterson

Series developed by Peggy Schmidt

LEE COUNTY LIBRARY
107 Hawkins Ave.
Sanford, NC 27330

Princeton, New Jersey

A New Century Communications Book

Other titles in this series include:

CARS
COMPUTERS
EMERGENCIES
FASHION
FITNESS
HEALTH CARE
KIDS
MUSIC
OFFICE
SPORTS
TRAVEL

Copyright © 1994 by Peggy Schmidt

All rights reserved. No part of this book may be reproduced, stored in a retrieval system, or transmitted, in any form or by any means—electronic, mechanical, photocopying, recording, or otherwise—except for citations of data for scholarly or reference purposes with full acknowledgment of title, edition, and publisher and written notification to Peterson's Guides prior to such use.

Library of Congress Cataloging-in-Publication Data

Peterson, Linda
    Entertainment / by Linda Peterson.
        p.   cm.—(Careers without college)
    "A New Century Communications book."
    ISBN 1-56079-352-X : $7.95
    1. Performing arts—Vocational guidance. 2. Broadcasting—
Vocational guidance. I. Title. II. Series.
PN1580.P45   1994
791'.023—dc 20   94-6948
                                       CIP

Art direction: Linda Huber
Cover photo: Bryce Flynn Photography
Cover and interior design: Greg Wozney Design, Inc.
Composition: Book Publishing Enterprises, Inc.
Printed in the United States of America
10 9 8 7 6 5 4 3 2 1

Text photo credits
Color photo graphics: J. Gerard Smith Photography
Page xiv: © AP/Wide World Photos, © Warner Bros. Inc.
Page 18: © Gabe Palmer, Palmer/Kane Inc., The Stock Market
Page 34: © Andy Caulfield, The Image Bank
Page 50: © Tom Martin, The Stock Market
Page 68: © G. & M. David de Lossy, The Image Bank

ABOUT THIS SERIES

Careers without College is designed to help those who don't have a four-year degree (and don't plan on getting one any time soon) find a career that fits their interests, talents and personality. It's for you if you're about to choose your career—or if you're planning to change careers and don't want to invest a lot of time or money in more education or training, at least not right at the start.

Some of the jobs featured do require an associate degree; others require only on-the-job training that may take a year, several months or only a few weeks. In today's world, with its increasingly competitive job market, you may eventually want to consider getting a two- or maybe a four-year college degree to move up in a field.

Each title in the series features five jobs in a particular industry or career area. Some of them are "ordinary," others are glamorous. The competition to get into certain featured occupations is intense; as a balance, we have selected jobs under the same career umbrella that are easier to enter. Some of the other job opportunities within each field will be featured in future titles in this series.

Careers without College has up-to-date information that comes from extensive interviews with experts in each field. The format of each book is designed for easy reading. Plus, each book gives you something unique: an insider's look at the featured jobs through interviews with people who work in them now.

We invite your comments about the series, which will help us with future titles. Please send your correspondence to: Careers without College, c/o Peterson's Guides, Inc., P.O. Box 2123, Princeton, NJ 08543-2123.

Peggy Schmidt has written about education and careers for 20 years. She is author of Peterson's best-selling *The 90-Minute Resume*.

ACKNOWLEDGMENTS

Many thanks to the following people who provided invaluable information and assistance:

Neale Baxter, Bureau of Labor Statistics, Washington, D.C.

Junior Bridge, Unabridged Communications, Alexandria, Virginia

Shelly Cagner, Arbitron, New York, New York

Joseph DiSante, Capital Cities/ABC, Inc., Los Angeles, California

Mark Fraterick, National Association of Broadcasters, Washington, D.C.

Bruce Ferguson, Cable Advertising Bureau, New York, New York

Cheryl Fuchs, ABC-TV Daytime Publicity, New York, New York

Edward J. Galizia Jr., The Art Institute of Fort Lauderdale, Fort Lauderdale, Florida

Margaret Gettings, Lyric Opera of Chicago, Chicago, Illinois

Diana Graves, The Art Institute of Atlanta, Atlanta, Georgia

Pam Lontos, Lontos Sales & Motivation, Laguna Hills, California

Laura Morandin, Radio Advertising Bureau, New York, New York

David Mortimer, Baker Winokur Ryder, Beverly Hills, California

David O'Ferrall, IATSE Local 487, Baltimore, Maryland

Guy Pace, Actors' Equity Association, New York, New York

Michele Pearce, Theatre Communications Group, New York, New York

Bronwyn Preston, Dennis Davidson Associates, Los Angeles, California

Phyllis Stark, *Billboard,* New York, New York

Mike Tiglio, NABET, Washington, D.C.

Diane Walden, American Women in Radio and Television, Washington, D.C.

Thanks also to the following "people finders" and "people suggesters": Katrina Allison, Jennifer Andrews, Marie Avery, Joanne Berg, Kathy Burkett, Mary Carter, Robyn Cohen, Bob Elson, Colleen Davis Gardephe, Susan Gordon, Gene Greenberg, Ted Greenwald, Melissa Burdick Harmon, Michele High, Patricia Hill, Dean Lamanna, Mark Morganstern, Peggy Neer, Robert S. Peterson, Connie Pettit, Gary Plumlee, Maricella Ramirez, Leslie Saltus, Tom Seligson, Michele Shapiro, Bill Spellman and Charles Wright.

WHAT'S IN THIS BOOK

Why These Entertainment Careers?	vi
Sheryl Lee Ralph on Success and Happiness in the Entertainment Business	viii
Famous Beginnings	xiii
Actor/Actress	1
Disc Jockey	19
Stagehand	35
Camera Operator	51
Time Salesperson	69
More Information Please	82
Will You Fit into the Entertainment World?	84
About the Author	90

ENTERTAINMENT

WHY THESE ENTERTAINMENT CAREERS?

Many people dream about getting into the entertainment business and achieving fame and fortune. They often have visions of stardom—on the screen or the stage or on the radio—yet have no clear sense of how a long-term career may unfold. One reason is that there's often no one clearly defined path to success.

In this book you'll find five entertainment careers discussed in detail:

- ❏ Actor/actress
- ❏ Disc jockey
- ❏ Stagehand
- ❏ Camera operator
- ❏ Time salesperson

Each of these fields is vital to the entertainment industry, and not one of them demands a college degree. As in most areas of the industry, the elements of success come down to talent, hard work, a great deal of luck, and sometimes—admittedly—who you know. What most of these careers have in common is that they're difficult to get into and highly competitive. Ambition and drive are essential.

On the creative front are actors and disc jockeys; both careers are among the most visible and glamorous in the field. But there are also many others whose contributions are critically important to the industry.

WHY THESE ENTERTAINMENT CAREERS?

Literally behind the scenes are the stagehands, who help performers in front of the curtain "make the magic happen" in the theater or on television. The camera operators in film and video use their artistic eye and knowledge of lighting to make actors look good on the big or small screen. Advertising salespeople tow the bottom line: bringing in the bucks for commercials that keep a radio or television station on the air.

In addition to updated information about each of these careers, each chapter includes interviews with people working in that field. They give you a highly personal, "hands on" sense of what it's really like and tell you why they enjoy coming to work every day.

People who are interested in this business tend to be committed to developing their potential; thus many do go to college. However, you find just as many for whom the pursuit of excellence leads from one project to the next, a real-life "school" of experiences that add up to a high degree of professionalism and artistic skill.

In pursuing any of these careers, you should put the goal of personal satisfaction before the hopes of financial reward. If the two happen to come together, you've struck gold. But remember that your motivation for entering this field may be all you'll have to sustain you when the going gets tough.

When the esteemed actor Robert Mitchum received a Lifetime Achievement Award from the American Theatre Arts Association, he made this comment in his acceptance speech: "My mother once told me, 'There are two kinds of people in this world—those who come to give, and those who come to "git." ' If you come to 'git,' think carefully. If you come to give, then by all means come! For this industry cries its need for every gift of the human spirit."

ENTERTAINMENT

SHERYL LEE RALPH

On Success and Happiness in the Entertainment Business

Sheryl Lee Ralph has it all—brains, beauty and talent—and she's done it all—acting, singing and dancing on stage, screen and television. Within months of graduating from Rutgers University at age 19 with a degree in English literature and theater arts, she tried her luck in Hollywood. Her film debut was a role in Sidney Poitier's 1977 film, *A Piece of the Action*. But finding film roles scarce, she moved back to New York, where she earned national fame—and a Tony nomination—for her performance as the lead singer in the hit Broadway musical *Dreamgirls*.

Ralph has had leading or featured roles in several television comedy series, including *It's a Living, Designing Women,* and her latest, *George,* in which she co-stars with George Foreman. In feature films, she earned critics' raves for her comic flair in *The Distinguished Gentleman,* opposite Eddie Murphy. Other films have included *The Mighty Quinn,* with Denzel Washington, *Sister Act II,* with Whoopi Goldberg, *Mistress,* with Robert De Niro, and *To Sleep With Anger,* with Danny Glover.

Behind the scenes, Ralph has her own production company, Island Girl Productions, and designs a line of children's clothing, Le Petit Etienne, named for her small son.

I've always had the desire to act and to sing. As a child my first acting role was in *The Miracle Worker* in summer stock in Connecticut. But I never thought performing would be my life; I always thought I would do something really "responsible" like become a doctor or lawyer. And I did enter Rutgers University as a premed student. But I quickly realized that a career in medicine was not for me—maybe it was that dead bunny in organic chemistry!

In college I won the American College Theater Festival acting scholarship. I placed as first runner-up in the Miss Black Teenage New York Pageant, where I had sung for the talent segment. One thing led to another, and I started winning money by performing and realized: This is something I LOVE. I was also an intern at the Negro Ensemble Company (NEC) in New York. I was the understudy for an Off Broadway play my acting teacher at NEC wrote, and that's how I got my Equity card.

One of the pageant judges owned a talent agency called Black Beauty, and that's how I got my first agent. I started doing national commercials, which were the bread and butter of my acting career for the first few years. I once did an AT&T commercial where I talked on the telephone while I stood on my head. You never know what kind of talent can help you get work!

ENTERTAINMENT

I've acted in theater, film and TV, and each is different. On the stage, there's that immediate response of the audience—you know right away what your work is like, and that's hard to replace. In television there is an audience at the taping, but there's also that net that lets you do it again if you need to. In film production, it's often "hurry up and wait" to shoot your scene. Then you get in there and do your ten seconds and that's it. Even if you want to concentrate on film or TV, you should understand and know the theater.

People sometimes ask about the qualities you need to make it as an entertainer. Typical answers are talent, perseverance and self-confidence, but in truth it's not always about those things. A lot of success in this business has to do with the right timing, the right look, the right agency, the right friend. Many people make it just because they knew the right person at the right time and had a certain quality, so I don't know if it's really perseverance that helped them. I also want to say you need self-confidence, but I know so many actors who don't have it and act *because* they find confidence in the creation of other characters.

I love when I'm able to create characters; I love when I'm able to make the unreal real. That's what I live to do, to give these words a life. It looks so easy to people, but it's not easy! Everybody thinks they can act, and I think that's because there are so many good actors who make it *seem* effortless. That's a testament to their craft and to their dedication. I hear people say things like "I didn't realize acting was this hard," and I think, What did you expect?

A lot of people interested in entertainment start out thinking that they want to be actors and discover that it's really not the right field for them. But there are so many other ways to be part of this business.

Especially in theater. The stage is a well-oiled machine. The actors depend on all the people backstage, the ones the audience never sees, to help them make it happen. For example, when *Dreamgirls* opened, it was momentous and historical in its use of props and lighting and sound. The actors were very dependent on stagehands to help us make the magic, because things had to happen very quickly. It's even more true today, with more emphasis on special effects and big spectacles on stage.

When you're acting in film or television, the camera operators are your "eyes." When you're in the scene, you can't necessarily see how the scene is going to "look." The camera operators and the director can help you get into the right light, make you look good, and help you be your better self.

Those of us who act in television series depend on the salespeople who sell air time to sponsors because their efforts help keep our show on the air. In fact, shows are sometimes chosen by networks because of the kind of advertisers they can draw.

In addition to acting, there's one other career in this book that I can really relate to. While I was in college I was a disc jockey on the campus station. I had the dinnertime slot, and friends would turn on my show in the college cafeteria. I played all kinds of music, and I had a great time! I also worked as a disc jockey for a time when I moved back to Jamaica, West Indies, where my mother lives.

New opportunities are always happening in this business. For example, there was a time when people looked down on acting on cable television or the idea of shopping via a cable network. That has changed. Major careers have been made with home shopping, and major personalities have been built with new types of programming. I remember when people said infomercials were not going to last.

One thing is constant. No matter which entertainment career you consider, you've *got* to love it. You've got to want it more than anything because it's so hard to make it and there's so much competition and so much rejection. It's called show business, and you've got to treat it as such. But in your heart you've got to remember that it is an art. You should be doing this because you love it, and you should be willing to sacrifice and even starve for a while. If you're not willing to do those things, it's not the business for you.

I always knew I was in this business to stay; I was never going to give up. I never, ever thought I wasn't going to make it. If anything, I thought those people who didn't hire me were crazy, and I felt that *they* weren't going to make it! But that's the kind of faith you've got to have in yourself.

FAMOUS BEGINNINGS

Casey Kasem, host of *Casey's Top Forty* and *Casey's Countdown,* syndicated pop music countdown shows heard by eight million people every week

At age 12 Kasem walked into a tiny mom-and-pop grocery store in his Detroit neighborhood. "It was a mess, with boxes stacked all over," he recalls. "I told the owner, 'If I clean it up, I can double your business for you.' I got hired the next day at 50 cents an hour. I took care of the beer and pop bottles, I made the produce as attractive as I could, I kept the shelves clean and neat—and most important, I made sure people could *get* to everything in the store!"

America's most famous radio personality had his first success behind a microphone in high school, where he belonged to the radio club and did a sports show. "I created my own sports announcing show and reported the action very much the way I report human interest stories today. I actually still have many handwritten reports that I did, re-creating the last minutes of big games."

Kasem's employer shared his pride in the young man whose radio career would go on to span four decades. "The grocery store owner put a little picture of me with a microphone just above the cash register, where everybody could see it. He and I had a great friendship through the years."

Michael Douglas, Oscar-winning actor/producer

This productive entertainer has always had a strong work ethic. In his first job, as a gas station attendant, he earned a Mobil Man of the Month citation for his efforts. Today, behind the scenes or in front of the cameras, he still strives to do his best—and has the awards to prove it. His production of *One Flew Over the Cuckoo's Nest* earned an Academy Award for Best Picture in 1975, and he won the Best Actor statuette in 1987 for his performance as a ruthless corporate raider in *Wall Street.*

ACTOR/ACTRESS

"I'd like to thank the members of the Academy . . ." Do you ever fantasize about winning the Oscar for Best Actor or Best Actress? Plenty of young people do. However, the odds against achieving steady work as an actor or actress—much less fame and fortune—are daunting. Success in the acting profession doesn't happen "overnight," and it may well not happen at all.

There's a reason why so many aspiring actors in New York and Los Angeles are waiters, taxi drivers and temporary secretaries: They need to pay the bills. It is estimated that 85 percent of actors are unemployed at any given time. And the millions of dollars earned by movie megastars is hardly the norm. The Screen Actors Guild reports that the average

ENTERTAINMENT

yearly income for film actors is $12,500. Stage performers belonging to Actors' Equity average $10,676; median earnings are only $5,200, and more than half have *no* earnings. (The term "actor" will include both men and women in this chapter.)

As in most areas of entertainment, success requires talent, hard work, good luck and good timing. Actors don't climb a standard ladder; they just get out there and perform. Typically they begin to learn their craft in amateur productions of plays and musicals (generally called community theater) or in nonprofit professional theater companies (called regional or repertory theater). Some land bit roles in low-budget, independently produced films or work as "extras" (nonspeaking, background roles) in television entertainment programs or major motion pictures. Others get noticed through their exposure in TV commercials.

Getting that first role involves sending your 8 x 10 picture and resume to casting agencies and production companies and learning what local stage, film or TV productions are in the works. It means trying out at "open" auditions that anyone can attend. It means striving to get a respected agent to represent you (in return for 10 percent of your earnings from roles the agent helps you obtain).

An audition for a dramatic role typically involves performing a two-minute monologue from a well-known play or reading a short scene from the work you're trying out for. For a musical audition, you're expected to sing a song or two and perhaps dance. As you perform, the show's casting director, producer, director and others evaluate your ability and potential for the role. If they like you, you get a "callback," and the list of contenders gets shorter and shorter until they make their choice.

Yet even if you are the classic "triple threat"—an actor/singer/dancer—you will have periods when you can't seem to get work. If you don't truly love performing, you'll become too disheartened over the endless uncertainty of making a living and will likely quit for a more stable career. Acting can be a tough, potentially heartbreaking business. As those who have "made it" often advise, if there's something else you want to do, do *that* instead. But if you simply can't imagine being anything but an actor, then go for it—and give it your all.

ACTOR/ACTRESS

Getting into the Field

What You Need to Know

- ❏ History of the theater
- ❏ Acting techniques and principles—the craft of acting
- ❏ How to read a script and analyze characters
- ❏ Basics of stage, film and TV production

Necessary Skills

- ❏ Ability to sing and dance extremely helpful
- ❏ Good speaking voice, clear diction and projection
- ❏ Excellent memory for learning lines
- ❏ Physical grace and agility—ability to "move well"
- ❏ Ability to apply your own makeup and style your hair
- ❏ Special talents, such as playing a musical instrument, very helpful; also puppetry or pantomime for children's theater
- ❏ Ability to mimic different accents helpful
- ❏ Good sense of comic timing and delivery very helpful

Do You Have What It Takes?

- ❏ Innate talent and the patience to learn the craft
- ❏ Ability to withstand frequent rejection; a "thick skin"
- ❏ Willingness to follow direction
- ❏ Ability to maintain concentration amid noise and distractions
- ❏ Team-player mentality
- ❏ Stamina, perseverance, determination
- ❏ High self-confidence; upbeat, "can do" attitude
- ❏ Reliability, punctuality
- ❏ No "stage fright" or inhibitions about public performing
- ❏ Flexibility (for relearning lines that often change in rehearsal)
- ❏ Sense of humor

ENTERTAINMENT

Physical Requirements

How you look often is *the* deciding factor in whether you get a role. The director may envision a short redhead, a well-muscled jock, a classic beauty or a girl-next-door type; if that's not you, you just won't get the job. Makeup artists can "age" an actor, but they cannot make anyone look significantly younger.

Education

A high school education is expected.

Licenses Required

None. But union membership is required for most speaking roles in film, television and professional theater. Performers on radio and videotaped TV programs (most sitcoms, daytime soaps and variety shows) belong to AFTRA, the American Federation of Television and Radio Artists. Actors who appear on film (motion pictures, most prime-time TV and commercials) join SAG, the Screen Actors Guild. Extras join the Screen Extras Guild. Actors in professional theater (Broadway, Off Broadway and regional theater nationwide) become members of Actors' Equity Association.

Job Outlook

Competition for jobs: extremely intense

Overall, television commercials are the greatest source of paid employment for actors. Television programs and motion pictures provide more roles than professional theater. In the next decade, actors should find more job opportunities due to the increase in film and theater production; the growth of cable television and TV syndication markets; foreign market demand for U.S. films; and the videocassette boom.

ACTOR/ACTRESS

◆ The Ground Floor

Entry-level job: film or TV extra or day performer, theater chorus member

◆ On-the-Job Responsibilities

Entry-Level and Experienced Actors

- ❏ Read scripts of films, TV shows or plays
- ❏ Decide how to interpret characters and confer with directors
- ❏ Memorize characters' lines and learn stage directions
- ❏ Practice movements, gestures, facial expressions
- ❏ Practice using or handling any props involved
- ❏ Work as a team with fellow actors, production crew, etc.
- ❏ Work with choreographers if dancing is required
- ❏ Get fitted for characters' wardrobe
- ❏ Rehearse, rehearse and rehearse

Acting in a motion picture or TV program is very different from working in live theater. In the latter, you perform the entire work in continuity; you must be "on" for two or three hours. In films there is a great deal of stop-and-go; scenes are shot separately and often out of sequence, and many "takes" may be required before the director is satisfied.

◆ When You'll Work

Acting is almost never a nine-to-five job. Principal players in weekly TV series and daytime dramas (soap operas) have the most predictable hours, working Monday through Friday. In the theater, actors generally work eight performances (six evenings and two afternoon matinees) for a 36-hour workweek. Before the show opens, however, the actors spend many more hours in rehearsals, which can last up to six weeks.

Film production is a highly concentrated effort. The workday can be 16 hours long. The actual filming ("principal photography") takes anywhere from three to five months.

ENTERTAINMENT

Time Off

Principal actors in TV series work the regular 22-week season, then generally are off from April through July.

Actors in TV soap operas (produced year-round, no reruns) earn paid vacation after a year. Film actors leave the production when their scenes are completed. In professional theater, principal actors appear in all performances for the duration of their contract unless they are unable to perform because of illness or injury. In long-running shows, actors get paid vacation.

Perks

- Opportunity to meet and work with celebrated actors
- Media attention, public recognition
- Invitations to film premieres, celebrity functions
- Frequently, first-class travel and accommodations, especially on commercial shoots
- Occasional "freebies" of clothes and merchandise

Who's Hiring

- Production companies for network television, cable, motion pictures and video
- Television and radio commercial production companies and advertising agencies, for on-screen roles and "voice-overs"
- Commercial theater (Broadway, Off Broadway and in big cities)
- Regional theater companies (about 400 in the U.S.)
- Dinner theaters (largely suburban operations)
- University theaters (affiliated with colleges, drama schools)
- Children's theaters (also called Theater for Young Audiences)
- Business theater (convention, sales conference performances)
- Summer stock theater (country and resort areas)
- Community theaters (generally all-amateur, but many hire professional "guest artists" for a production)

ACTOR/ACTRESS

❑ Producers of entertainment for cruise ships, gambling casinos, resorts, state fairs, etc.
❑ Amusement parks
❑ Educational/training film production companies
❑ Producers of "books on tape"

Places You'll Go

Beginners and experienced actors: Great potential for travel

Obviously, when a show goes "on the road," much travel is involved. The national touring company of a hit Broadway show may remain in a major city for many weeks, while a "bus and truck" tour usually plays in a different small town every few nights. Motion picture production often goes on location to exotic places.

Surroundings

An actor may perform in a plush, air-conditioned theater or in a dusty church basement, in a state-of-the-art television studio or on a remote movie location in all kinds of weather. Stage and TV studio lights can be very hot, which can dry out a performer's hair and skin. Theater dressing rooms may be spacious and private or shared and cramped, with few amenities. In film, an actor can spend tedious hours in a tiny trailer waiting to be called as production crews get ready for each scene.

Dollars and Cents

Members of actors' unions are guaranteed a minimum salary (called "scale"), though their agents may negotiate much higher fees. Current film and TV minimums are $485 per day, or $1,685 for a five-day week; general extras get $65 a day. Broadway performers earn a minimum of $950 a week; Off Broadway theaters pay $340 to $579 a week. Touring stage performers get extra because they must pay for their lodging. Minimum weekly salaries in regional theaters throughout the country range from $428 to $547.

Actors also earn money from "residuals" when a

ENTERTAINMENT

motion picture is sold to television or the videotape market, when a TV program is rebroadcast, or when a commercial is long-running. When a job is over, many actors cannot get unemployment benefits because they didn't work long enough to qualify for them.

Moving Up

Success, of course, means better and bigger roles, more money and more opportunity to work with respected actors, producers and directors. If and when actors stop performing, they may become directors, producers, stage managers, casting directors, agents or acting coaches or move into playwriting or screenwriting.

Where the Jobs Are

Most auditions for television, film and major theater roles take place in Los Angeles and New York City. The Los Angeles area remains production king for motion pictures and prime-time TV, though Miami, Chicago, San Francisco, Dallas, Houston, Atlanta, Denver and Toronto are also production centers. (All states and most major cities have a film commission that promotes regional movie production.) Soap operas are divided between Los Angeles and New York. The greatest percentage of TV commercials are produced in California; the rest are made mainly in New York and Chicago. Broadway still dominates the commercial stage, but the more than 400 nonprofit professional theaters across the U.S. now provide the most acting jobs in theater.

Training

Dramatic arts training is available at specialty schools and actors' studios, most of which are in New York City, Los Angeles and other large cities. Schools offering associate degrees in theater arts/drama are listed in *Peterson's Guide to Two-Year Colleges*.

ACTOR/ACTRESS

There are more acting opportunities for women in commercials and television programs than in films. According to a 1990 SAG survey, women had 46 percent of television roles and 30 percent of movie roles. Women account for 43 percent of SAG's 75,000 members and 47 percent of the 37,000 members of Actors' Equity.

◆ The Male/Female Equation

◆ Making Your Decision: What to Consider

The Bad News

❏ No guarantee of success or steady income
❏ Talent may not be enough
❏ You may struggle for years to get a major role
❏ Hours can be irregular; night and weekend rehearsals
❏ Anxiety-producing rejection and periodic unemployment

The Good News

❏ Excitement, recognition, possible world travel
❏ Thrill of live performance before a theater audience
❏ Fulfillment through artistic expression
❏ Possibility (however small) of fame and fortune
❏ Fresh challenge with every job

ENTERTAINMENT

What It's Really Like

Jessica Collins, 23, actress, ABC-TV's *Loving*, New York, New York
Years in the field: four

How did you break into this business?
In 1988 I won Miss Teen New York and was first runner-up in Miss Teen USA. When I won Miss Teen New York, one of the judges was a big commercial casting director in New York. She called me in to audition for a commercial, and I got it! I didn't have an agent, so the casting director called another pageant judge, who was an agent, and asked if she'd represent me. Two weeks after my high school graduation, I moved to New York City by myself. The casting director introduced me to different agents and gave me the names of acting coaches and teachers to look into. She was just always there for me.

How did you support yourself at first?
As a waitress. My other "job" was going on auditions. I was freelancing with about nine different agents because the casting director had told me not to sign with anyone till I'd worked with all of them and saw who sent me out the most.

I was going on auditions mostly for commercials, but also for films, soaps and other television. I had just one big commercial, and the rest were tiny parts. I also did a bit of "extra" work, I was a day player on a soap, and that was it.

How did you deal with the daily rejection at auditions?
It was hourly rejection! Sometimes I'd think, I've got it, the casting director loved me—and then I wouldn't get it. But I'd tell myself, It's nice to know you were close; maybe the casting director will use you next time.

How did you get the job on the soap opera *Loving*?
When I was 20 I screen-tested for the role of a 16-year-old on *Loving*. They didn't think I looked 16, but the ABC people liked me enough to create (the role of) Dinah, who's a bit older, for me.

What do you like most about this business?
I love performing, even the preparation for it. This is my "college" right here. It's terrific, and I get paid for it.

What don't you like about it?
Unfortunately, most of the time your look is what gets you in more than your talent, so you have to concentrate on your look. Your hair has to be in good condition, and you have to watch your weight. If you get a pimple, forget it. Then there's the business of promoting yourself. You have to meet all the "right" people. You have to go to parties to network, and it's not always fun. And sometimes a casting director can be a real creep.

What advice would you give aspiring actors?
Really, really think about whether this is what you want to do. You can't get into acting to be a "movie star." You've got to learn the business and learn your craft. And you've got to have a plan—both short- and long-term goals. I planned for years. I'd saved my pageant money and looked for an apartment six months before I moved here.

What is your long-term goal?
Films. So I see myself moving to L.A. and trying it out.

ENTERTAINMENT

David DeWitt, 30, film and stage actor, New York, New York
Years in the field: 11

How did you get into this business?
After graduating from high school (in Birmingham, Alabama), I was working in a bookstore. I know this sounds odd, but one night I just had a realization—almost like a voice telling me "You are to be an actor." I had no doubts then and never have.

What was your first role?
In the chorus of a local theater production of *Li'l Abner*. I'd always sung in the church choir, and I'd always danced at local dances, so I had no trouble with the steps. I was paid $50 a week for four weeks of rehearsal and the two-week run.

Then I got a chorus role in our community theater's brand-new musical. The musical director was from New York, and he told me I should move there and pursue this professionally.

Did you run home and pack?
Oh, no. I was scared to death. I decided to try to do a few more shows and see how I felt after that. Then I moved to Atlanta to earn more money—I worked in a mental ward as a psychiatric assistant. After a year I finally decided it was time to go to New York. I called the musical director and asked if his offer to use his apartment was still open, and he said yes. I found out later that he has helped dozens of people get started this way. I got a job as a waiter, then I got my own apartment sublet, and I started getting some work as a film extra.

How did you find work without an agent?
I read *The Hollywood Reporter* to find out about movies in production. I'd look to see who was casting a film, then I'd send the casting agency my picture. I only got extra work; it's very hard to get seen for principal roles without a big agent.

Were you studying acting?
I've never studied acting. At that time I felt that it was something that came naturally or not at all. It helps some people, but I'm not one of them. I once audited an acting class (observing without participating), and I was bored to death.

I got a role in an HBO film and thought it would hold me over, so I quit the restaurant job. But I ran out of money. I was walking dogs to earn money. Then my lease ran out, and I had no place to stay. I was lucky to land the job of sexton (someone who cares for church property) at my church, because an apartment came with it.

There's a great group of artists and actors at the church. An actor friend, Bill Phillips, and I put on a benefit performance of the play *Greater Tuna*. People loved it, and we decided to write a play about the homeless problem. A church member was running a conference on social action and asked if we could write a short play about a social issue—unbelievable timing. We wrote a one-act, two-actor play, *Outside the Window*.

We performed it at the conference and wound up touring with the play for about a year. It was filmed and aired internationally over a satellite network; we were nominated for an award. That got us a lot of recognition. People said, "You should be in films." So in 1988 I moved to L.A.

Did you get an agent then?
No. And in L.A. you need an agent to go to the bathroom. Everything there is by appointment, which is controlled by agents, whereas in New York there are so many independent films and open auditions that you can get a reasonable amount of work without an agent.

By a fluke I got a radio commercial, which got me into the actors' unions. I ended up working as a receptionist for an entertainment company, and a casting director there got me into quite a few auditions. It would come down to two (actors), then to one, and it wasn't me.

Why did you return to New York?
After two years I decided that I really hated L.A. I came back in 1990 to be with my girlfriend, who's now my wife.

ENTERTAINMENT

I've done several films since then. It's been extra work or stand-in work (physically doubling for a star while lights and cameras are set for each film scene), but it's been steady. I've been in several Off Off Broadway musicals, and I've gotten some callbacks for Broadway. I'm also working for myself now. I'm an artist, and I design and hand-paint my own greeting cards. A major supermarket chain is test-marketing them.

Do you think you'll stay in acting?
Yes. I believe it's what I'm meant to do. But I'm to the point now where I feel that if I'm going to make it, I'm going to have to write and produce my own projects.

Mary Tanner, 30,
actress,
Nashville, Tennessee
Years in the field: ten

How did you get interested in acting?
During high school (in Nashville) I got involved in children's theater, and I really enjoyed it. Then I went to Boston University for two years in a B.F.A. program until I thought, nobody in the business cares if you have a B.F.A. or not. Then I got a part on a PBS children's series. The producers encouraged me to go to New York. So I did.

How did you get an agent?
My PBS contacts recommended me to a few agents. I went on auditions and started getting good feedback. I was supporting myself as a retail salesclerk. After eight months I signed with a very good agent, and a month later I got lead roles in two "teenage" motion pictures. I was 21, but I was able to play young. It was great experience; I got to work with Patty Duke and John Glover. Then I got a TV-movie role.

In the winter of 1986 I went to L.A. for pilot season (when TV's new fall shows are chosen). I was auditioning all the time, and I was incredibly focused and self-confident. I wound up getting cast as a 15-year-old in a sitcom pilot called *The Cavanaughs*. We shot the pilot in April; I was already back in New York when I learned CBS had picked it up. The producers offered me money to move to L.A.

Were you willing to relocate?
Yes. After three years I was tired of New York. And, as my agent liked to put it, I was "hot." Before *The Cavanaughs* began regular shooting, I got a part in an after-school TV special. I thought it was going to be this good all the time.

We did the sitcom for about two and a half years, on and off, because they kept taking us off the air. Then the network put it on "hold." We were paid, but I couldn't take any other jobs, so essentially I lost my momentum. Finally the show was canceled. For the next two years, I sort of fell through the cracks. I was getting too old to play teenagers. I wasn't totally out of work, but I was just doing my last few acting jobs for the money, and that's not why I became an actor.

How did you deal with rejection?
When I was strong and confident, I just knew I could keep going. But when things got difficult, my self-confidence went down the tubes. I started to feel that I should quit, despite the positive things other people were saying to me.

Nothing was going right. My association with my New York agent was ending; my personal life was bad; my career was not working out. My whole focus just fell apart, and when you lose your focus, it comes across in your work. So I went back home. I didn't know if I could handle all the rejection.

What have you been doing in Nashville?
I got involved in theater here. And sure enough, after five months I got my little (acting) bug back. I felt more confident and ready to handle L.A. again. So I went back for pilot season and got a part in a TV movie. After that job I came back home and did more theater. I was having great fun. And then I fell in love! So I decided not to go back to L.A. But in the fall my agent called and told me I'd gotten a guest role on TV's *Murder, She Wrote* because she'd sent them my (demo) tape. So I flew to L.A., worked three days and made five thousand dollars, then came back home again.

ENTERTAINMENT

So you were jet-lagged but happy, with no more doubts?
Yes. It's taken awhile, but I'm realizing that I'm good at what I do. When I went back for *Murder, She Wrote*, I hadn't acted for several months. But I got onto that set, face to face with Angela Lansbury, and did a great job. It hit me all of a sudden that, after ten years, I *know* how to work in front of a camera. I have a lot to learn, but I know I'm a professional, and it was the first time I really felt good about saying that to myself. I know now that I can hack it, whether it's here or there.

What do you like most about acting?
Performing and rehearsing gives me a little "buzz," a satisfaction I don't get with anything else.

What do you like least?
The waiting and the rejection and the competition.

Do you have any advice for aspiring actors?
You have to be really sure this is what you want. If you believe you can do it, do it. But if it's not feeling right anymore, then walk away. When a friend of mine decided to stop acting, she said it felt wonderful, like a huge weight had been lifted from her. But when I decided not to act, all I felt was sadness. Your heart will tell you if you're doing the right thing.

ACTOR/ACTRESS

DISC JOCKEY

Radio can be an intimate medium, even though thousands or millions of listeners may be tuned in. Disc jockeys (also called deejays, DJs or jocks) are the friendly, familiar voices that people may feel they almost know personally. DJs play various types of music, give updates on the news, traffic and weather, and generally provide their listeners with entertainment and companionship.

And people do listen—for over three hours every day. Radio is in 99 percent of American homes, with an average of five radios per household. Most listeners choose one station over another because of the music.

Most commercial radio stations today specialize in one programming format—usually a specific kind of music

ENTERTAINMENT

aimed at listeners of a certain type and age. In 1993 radio's most listened-to formats were country music, adult contemporary (also called soft or "lite" rock), news/talk, Top 40 (also called CHR or contemporary hit radio) and album rock (a mix of current and "oldies" rock). There are many other formats and even subspecialties of those.

The DJ's role largely depends on the format. Top 40 stations, especially on the morning commuter "drive-time" shows, tend to emphasize "personality" disc jockeys. Between discs, these often zany entertainers may do comedy bits and make sharp observations on topical issues. At stations featuring "easy listening" beautiful music, soft rock or jazz, DJs typically are more low-key. They have a smooth and relaxed delivery, spend much more time playing music than talking and rarely, if ever, say anything controversial. In most markets DJs no longer choose the music on their show but follow a "playlist" selected by the station's music director or program director, usually with the help of a computer.

At small stations in particular, DJs are expected to be multitalented: In addition to their on-air duties, they may have to sell ads, write and produce commercial or promotional copy and even operate the broadcast transmitter. But for all DJs, one job aspect is the same: They must always be "on." If they're having a bad day, their listeners must never suspect it.

Getting that first job usually means making an audio tape (called an air check) of your on-air delivery and sending it to radio station program directors. The tapes are usually short—perhaps only five minutes. The idea is to show your voice and style of delivery in music commentary, commercials and news headlines.

If you're called for an interview, you may be asked to read aloud news or commercial copy. If you are hired, you probably will not get to the microphone right away. Your first job is often as a "gofer" or assistant or, even more likely, as an unpaid intern. If you perform well and show you've learned how the station works, you may be considered when an on-air opening occurs.

If you dream about a job on the "jukebox of the air," read on.

DISC JOCKEY

◆ Getting into the Field

What You Need to Know

- ❑ Basics of radio broadcasting, station operation
- ❑ The current music scene and performers
- ❑ Specifics of a station's music format
- ❑ Current events for on-air commentary
- ❑ How to operate the control console (basic sound controls on the radio board)

Necessary Skills

- ❑ Excellent vocabulary, good grammar, correct pronunciation, clear diction
- ❑ Ability to think on your feet and ad-lib
- ❑ Strong writing skills (for DJ's script and commercial or news copy)
- ❑ Good sense of comic timing and delivery very helpful

Do You Have What It Takes?

- ❑ Self-confidence
- ❑ Ability to express your thoughts clearly
- ❑ A relaxed, friendly manner
- ❑ Ability to work under deadline pressure
- ❑ Ability to project authority and confidence
- ❑ Punctuality, reliability
- ❑ Sense of humor

Physical Requirements

- ❑ A voice that has a pleasing pitch and timbre

Education

A high school diploma is required.

ENTERTAINMENT

Licenses Required

Disc jockeys often are required to operate the radio broadcast transmitter. To do so they must obtain a Restricted Radiotelephone Operator's License from the Federal Communications Commission. A test is no longer required.

At large stations in the biggest cities, disc jockeys may have to join the talent union, AFTRA (the American Federation of Television and Radio Artists).

Job Outlook

Competition for jobs: extremely intense

There continue to be many more job seekers than jobs in the broadcasting field. In many markets, an increasing amount of a station's programming is syndicated (rather than produced by the station) or even completely automated, which means less need for "live" DJs. But there is high job turnover in this field, especially at small stations as DJs leave for bigger markets. New stations are always being licensed, creating job opportunities.

A word about markets: The bible of the radio industry is published by the Arbitron Company, which rates radio stations' listenership—audience "shares"—in 260 markets. The top 40 markets are metropolitan areas with populations of more than a million.

The Ground Floor

Entry-level job: disc jockey

DISC JOCKEY

Playing records (now compact discs or magnetic tape cartridges rather than vinyl LPs) and running the board is part of the DJ's job except at the biggest stations, where an engineer likely will do such tasks.

Entry-Level and Experienced Disc Jockeys

- Before going on-air, check music list and make sure tapes/CDs are ready
- Introduce music selections and artists
- Introduce or present news/weather/traffic updates
- Read commercials
- Identify station and dial position at regular intervals
- Make informal comments about music or topical issues, or follow a prepared script
- May take calls from listeners requesting songs
- May interview guest music artists during show
- Keep program log of all elements aired during broadcast (music selections, commercials, station promos)
- At small station, may set up microphones and tape players
- At small station, may operate radio transmitter, write advertising copy, sell air time
- Often make public appearances on behalf of radio station at sports events, charity benefits, etc. (for which there is usually additional pay)

Most radio stations broadcast 18 to 24 hours a day, seven days a week. Disc jockeys generally work a 40-hour week, possibly over six days, with on-air shifts ranging from three to six hours. A morning drive-time show airs from 5 or 6 A.M. to 10 or 11 A.M.; the midday show from 10 A.M. to 3 P.M.; the afternoon show from 3 to 7 P.M.; the evening show from 7 P.M. to midnight; and the overnight show from midnight to 5 A.M.

◆ **On-the-Job Responsibilities**

◆ **When You'll Work**

ENTERTAINMENT

Time Off

Eight paid holidays annually is the general standard. A new hire may be eligible for one week's vacation after six months of employment. However, during the nearly three-month-long Arbitron ratings periods (a station may be rated once or twice a year or more), vacations are frowned upon.

Perks

- Possibility of meeting famous recording artists
- Possibility of free admission to concerts and music events
- Merchandise discounts or freebies from advertisers
- Possibility that you'll be considered a local celebrity and do local "remotes"
- Trips to national conventions (the station often pays for these)

Who's Hiring

- Local AM and FM commercial radio stations
- Public FM stations (called noncommercial or educational stations)
- State and regional radio networks
- National radio networks
- Armed Forces Radio and Television (many civilians are employed at these stations)
- Advertising agencies (for commercial voice-overs)

Places You'll Go

Beginners and experienced DJs: Little potential for travel

Occasionally, a station may broadcast a show from a "remote" location, for a community or a sponsor-related event within the broadcast area.

DISC JOCKEY

Surroundings

A disc jockey's environment may range from a modern, well-lighted, air-conditioned, soundproof studio to a renovated basement with old facilities. Studio quarters can be tight and loaded with equipment. Except for big stations, where engineers sometimes work with them, DJs are alone in the studio; on the overnight shift, a DJ may well be the only person in the building.

Dollars and Cents

A 1993 salary survey for the industry publication *Radio & Records* (*R&R*) revealed that morning DJs earned an average of $80,862; the midday talent, $39,619; the afternoon talent, $49,400; the evening talent, $31,498, and the overnight talent, $23,049. It should be remembered, however, that these are averages of *all* market sizes; the smallest markets pay much less (and the top 15 markets pay much more). There are also very wide ranges among music formats. A morning DJ at a contemporary hits station in the largest markets averages $146,900, while the morning personality at a classical station in the same size markets averages $64,500. Top DJs—typically the "morning personalities" in fiercely competitive major markets who have proved that they can attract a big audience—earn six-figure salaries.

Moving Up

Changing jobs usually means changing towns, especially in small markets. However, many DJs happily remain big fish in medium-market ponds rather than continually moving to bigger markets. Only a very few ever get a nationally syndicated program like those of Casey Kasem, Shadoe Stevens and Rick Dees. Some DJs move into specialized areas, such as sportscasting or all-talk shows. Some have very profitable careers doing TV commercials. DJs who eventually leave on-air work may become program directors or general managers of a radio station.

ENTERTAINMENT

Where the Jobs Are

At the end of 1993, there were 11,500 AM and FM radio stations in the U.S. Virtually every town in America boasts at least one radio station. The most opportunities—and heaviest competition—are in the top ten markets: New York City (more than 80 stations), Los Angeles, Chicago, San Francisco, Philadelphia, Detroit, Washington, D.C., Dallas, Boston and Houston.

Training

Many community and junior colleges offer associate degree programs in broadcasting. Vocational/technical schools throughout the U.S. provide shorter programs and grant certificates. The latter schools vary in quality of instruction and facilities, so you should always check to see if the school is accredited by its state Department of Education or the Career College Association (formerly the National Association of Trade and Technical Schools). Some vocational broadcasting schools are listed in the *Broadcasting & Cable Yearbook* under "Education."

The Male/Female Equation

In 1993, according to the Census Bureau, 17 percent of the nation's 53,000 broadcast announcers were women.

Making Your Decision: What to Consider

The Bad News
- Very low pay to start
- Little job security
- Irregular hours common for entry-level DJs
- Frequent relocations can be hard on your personal life
- Need for perfect timing on-air can be stressful

The Good News
- Fast-paced, energetic environment
- Thousands of people are "your" listeners
- Satisfaction of creative work every day
- Casual dress on the job
- Potential to make big money

WHAT IT'S REALLY LIKE

Cathy Martindale, 39,
disc jockey, WSM-FM,
TV host, *Video PM,*
The Nashville Network,
Nashville, Tennessee
Years in the field: 20

How did you break into this business?
I was getting tired of studying pre-law when I saw a commercial for a "learn to be a disc jockey" course and thought it sounded like fun; it's theater of the mind. I had once planned to be an actress but felt I couldn't take the rejection.

The country radio station I listened to, KSCS in Dallas–Fort Worth, didn't have an opening; I told them I was coming over anyway. They asked me to read news copy; I was on the air in two weeks. I did a farm show from 5:30 to 6 A.M. on the AM station, then worked in the FM station from 6 A.M. to 3 P.M. I quit college shortly after I started. Within 18 months I became the program director, and the station went to number one. I was 21 and the only female broadcast manager in the whole [parent] company.

ENTERTAINMENT

How did you get to Nashville?
I stayed at KSCS five years, then quit in 1979 over salary. I went into the house-building business as a general contractor. But I kept doing a Sunday show on KBOX in Dallas. I also went to Nashville for country music conventions. At a seminar in 1983 I was offered the music director job at WSM AM-FM (in Nashville) and took it.

Five days a week I was in management, and Sundays I went on-air. I did that two years, then went back on-air full time to do the afternoon shift here. I was also working part time on TV at The Nashville Network (TNN) as a substitute announcer. We're all the same company—Opryland USA is WSM radio, the Grand Old Opry, TNN, and Opryland amusement park. I left in 1988 and went on the road to sell T-shirts for country music artist Billy Joe Royal.

That seems like an odd career move. What made you do it?
It's normal to get burned out and take time out. I loved the travel; we were on the road 25 days a month for a year and a half and traveled to every state but Alaska and Vermont and all over Canada. Seeing America gave me a better perspective on how to relate what I do on radio and TV. I *know* the people who are listening, watching and buying this music.

I worked on-air for WSM, if they needed me, whenever I came off the road. Then in 1990 I got the offer to do *Video PM*. I now have two shows on TNN—I also do *Country Beat* on Saturdays. Until recently my dog was my cohost. She got more fan mail than I did. Then in 1991, I came back to radio to do this show, *Karl and Cathy in the Morning*. So basically I have two full-time jobs, radio and TV. I also do a lot of freelance commercial work. I've done about 1,600 TV commercials, mostly for automobile dealers.

What do you like most about being a DJ?
It's a creative outlet for me. On the air, we also create a persona. We play on things that happen to us. Another plus is that listeners get to be your family. Country listeners are very loyal. I'm pleased to say that we are number one or two all the time according to Arbitron, and we've been in the top three for ten years.

What do you like least?
I get up about 4:30 A.M. to do the morning show. I can't force myself to sleep early, so I'm constantly sleep-deprived. Also, there's job insecurity. You never know if there's going to be a corporate takeover or a new program director or general manager, or if the owner's wife won't like you for some reason. You can never quite feel you've got everything under control because it can all be yanked away from you at any time. I say that even though I've never been fired or laid off.

What advice would you give aspiring DJs?
A big part of my success was not only my persistence and determination but my willingness to work for less than I should have been paid, just to get my foot in the door. So do whatever you can to get in, then work in there and always do more than is expected. Learn how the other departments—sales, promotion, engineering—work.

Kelly Nash, 26,
disc jockey, WKCI-FM,
New Haven, Connecticut
Years in the field: nine

What is your current position?
I'm the evening DJ on the number one station in New Haven, which plays a Top 40 format. I'm also the operations assistant, which means I help oversee sales, programming and promotions. I'm also program director for our AM affiliate.

How did you get interested in this career?
My cousin is a DJ in Los Angeles, and I always thought it was a cool way to make a living. In my senior year of high school, I got an internship at WPLR in New Haven. After I graduated, I got hired as a promotions assistant at KISS in Hartford. They let me run the prerecorded syndicated shows, like Casey Kasem. During the local break, I'd push buttons for the commercials and then run the jingles back into the program. After about five months they also let me fill in on the overnight for vacationing DJs.

Is that a usual way to get on the air?
Yes. Nobody wants to do overnight; you know no one's listening. At the same time I was also starting to do the 6 P.M. to midnight show on a small country station. Sometimes I was working 20 hours a day.

I was also writing a lot of freelance comedy bits for the American Comedy Network. If they used it, they'd pay $50 for a fake commercial or $100 for a song parody. It got to where I was making five or six hundred a week from that.

Anyway, the afternoon KISS jock went to Cleveland (Ohio), and I kept in touch, sending him comedy bits for free. When he moved to the morning show, he got me hired as his sidekick. So at age 19 I was cohost of a morning show in a big market. I was making $35,000, had my picture on city billboards and even got a free condo as part of the deal.

Wasn't that kind of success unusually fast?
Too fast. We did horribly for a number of reasons, one of which was that I was in over my head. After about a year, the station was sold and the new owners fired everybody. Then I went to a Lexington, Kentucky, station and did 7 P.M. to midnight. I got fired again in less than three months. I was miserable because they didn't understand my "creative genius." I was doing things that just didn't work in the Bible Belt.

I went back to Connecticut, to a small country station. I did a year on midday, and then they made me promotion director as well. We quadrupled our ratings—and the general manager fired me. He'd never liked me.

I quit my next job at a station in Vermont; the format wasn't my style. I came home and became manager of a jewelry store. I was making good money, but I wasn't happy.

Did you miss the microphone?
Oh yeah. Every time I turned on the radio I'd think, I should be doing this again. Then one day the guy who was programming KC (WKCI) called and asked if I'd consider doing their early Sunday show, from 3 A.M. to 8 A.M. I said

sure. I'd work at the store on Saturday till 9 P.M., then go home, nap, go to the station, do the show and sleep all day Sunday. After a while KC offered me $7 an hour to do the Saturday and Sunday "beach patrol"—driving the van to beaches and giving out prizes, etc. I had to quit my store job and move back in with my mom, but I decided to come back to radio.

How did you make that happen?
Even though I only worked weekends, I hung around the station every day. I told the sales staff, "If you're ever in a bind and need a DJ for an appearance, please consider me—let me show you what I can do." I was still only 21. Finally, one Saturday night I was asked to fill in for a DJ at a teen club. I worked the crowd, and afterward the club owner called the station and said he wanted me from now on. All the salespeople heard about it, and in two weeks I had two more regular gigs. Then I started getting remotes, and soon I was making $600 to $800 a week off these appearances. At summer's end I was hired as producer for the morning show. About eight months later the evening jock left, and I came back on-air full time.

What do you like most about being a DJ?
For four hours, my only job is to have fun. And I do. How could I not? Hundreds of people are calling me, wanting to tell me a joke or get in funny conversations.

What do you like least?
The fact that radio stations are being bought by people who don't know what they're doing. They're also so leveraged out that they need to make money, which means they can't risk a failure, and that has really put us in a creative and financial bind. Salaries are dropping. Maybe five percent of all DJs are making good money. The average salary is in the low 20s.

What advice do you have for aspiring DJs?
Get an internship. If you're good, they'll very likely create something for you. Work hard and make as many friends as possible. If you stick with it, something good will come out of it. Maybe not in two years or even ten, but it'll happen.

ENTERTAINMENT

Ron James, 24,
disc jockey, WFAS-FM,
White Plains, New York
Years in the field: three

How did you break into this business?
I was studying broadcasting at a community college and working on the campus radio station. Sue Richard, a DJ at WFAS, called the college station one day looking for an intern to help on her weekly dedication show, and I said, "Me me me!" Every Friday night I'd answer the song request line and pull all her music for her and all the commercials. It's a soft rock format here.

At my request Sue started critiquing tapes from my college radio show. Then the WFAS program director listened to my tape and put me on the board for a weekly satellite show called *Super Gold*. All I had to do was watch the board, occasionally give the station ID, then go on the air every hour and do the weather for 22 seconds. Eventually that helped me get fill-ins for the weekend overnight shift.

When did you get your own show?
In mid-1990 the regular overnight DJ left. That's when they hired me to replace her and to be the public service director for both WFAS-FM and WFAS-AM. Even though I'd done the show as a fill-in, I was really nervous my first night. Now it was *my* show, and I didn't want to screw up! I got the hang of it and learned to relax.

During my shift I'm all alone in the station. There used to be someone in the studio next door doing the overnight on the AM station, but they got a computer automation system for that shift, and now the computer does everything.

What do you do on a typical day?
I get here about 7 P.M. and go through all the mail that contains public service announcements. I decide what will go on the air and on which station. Then I go into production. The creative director gives me commercials to do. I may just have to cart it up (tape it onto a cartridge), but sometimes I also produce it. That means picking out the music

and sound effects and figuring out a character voice for it if necessary, then mixing it all.

At midnight I go on the air. I have little preparation for the show because I don't have a lot of time to talk. I've got 55 minutes of music to play every hour, and there are very few commercials on overnight. I read the (transmitter) meters for the AM and FM stations. Every three hours I check the antenna current and voltage and write it on the log.

What do you like most about being a DJ?
Just being in the business, being on the other side of the radio. Playing music and talking on the air is fun for me.

What's the down side?
There is absolutely no job security in radio. I could come in one day and the station could have switched formats, say to country, and I'd either have to deal with that or go somewhere else. Another one of those computers could be thrown on for the FM overnight and I could be fired. And the money early on is not great, especially at a small market like this. Also, when you work at night it's hard to have a social life.

What achievements are you most proud of so far?
The production work. That's really what I want to do—voice-overs on commercials, character voices, maybe cartoons.

What advice do you have for aspiring DJs?
Take some radio production courses so you learn the technical aspects of radio, take English courses, study voice and diction. Other than working at a radio station, getting an internship is the A number one important thing. Volunteer and see what happens. And be patient. You won't become a star overnight.

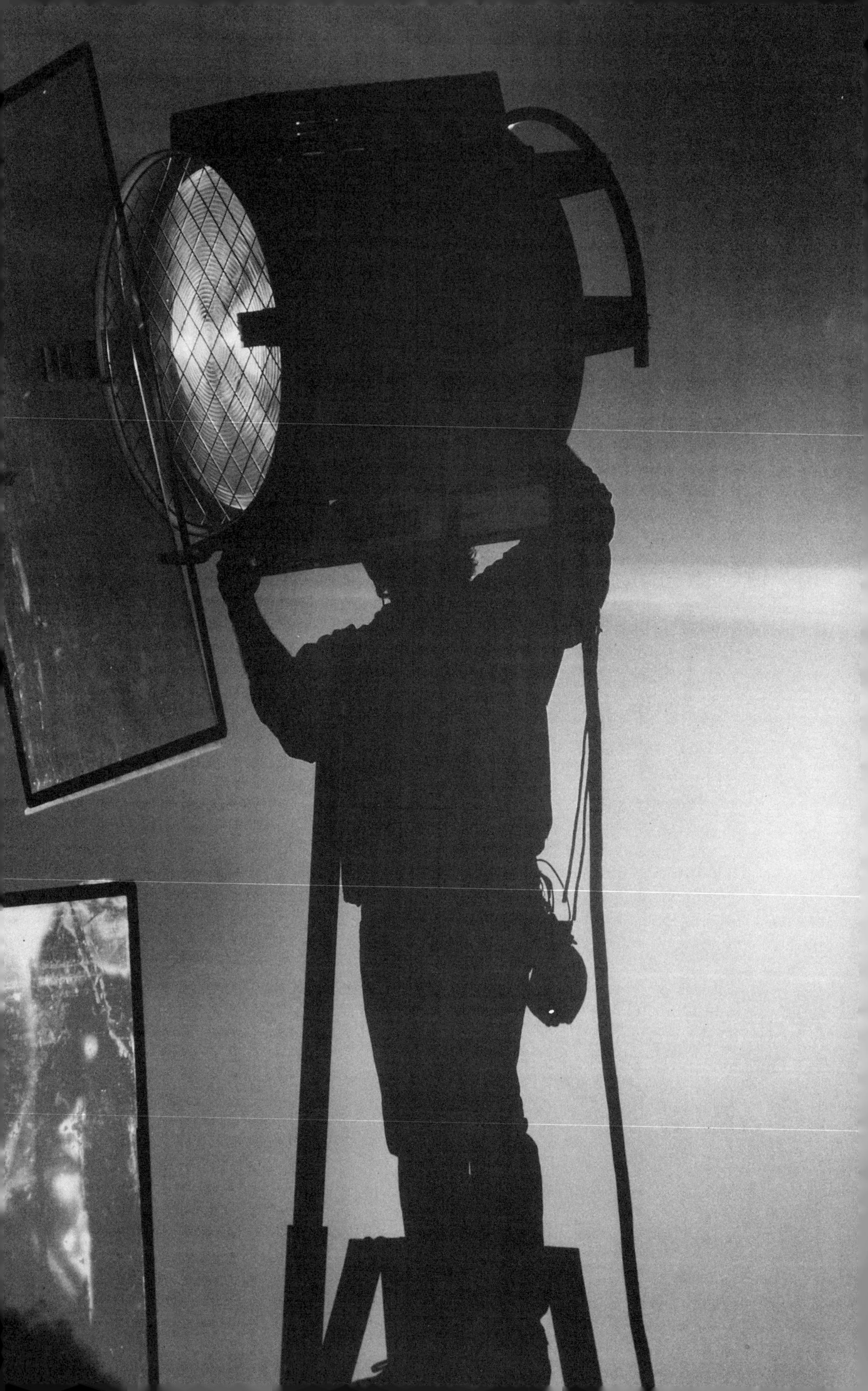

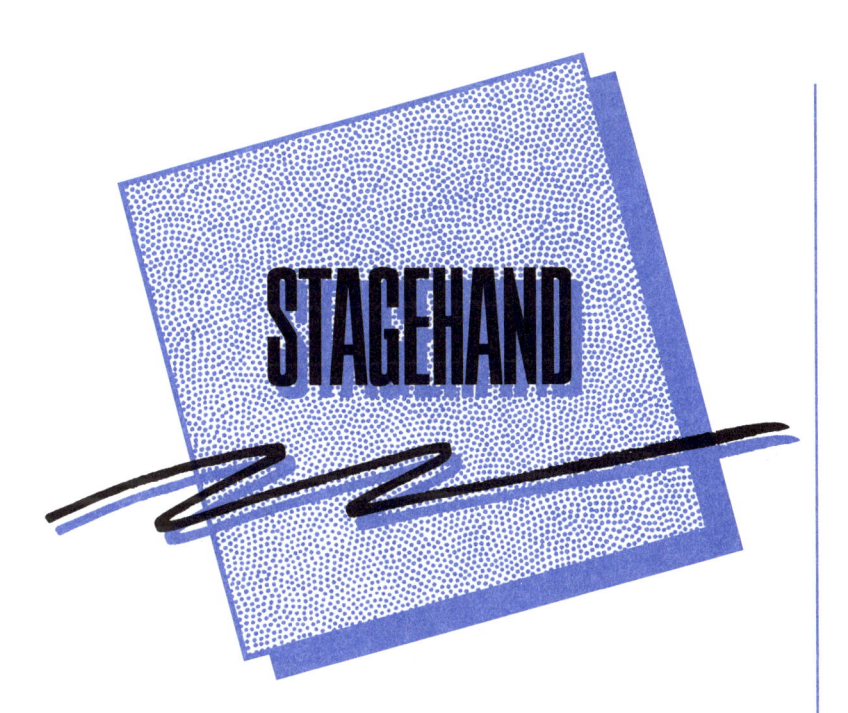

There are many people whose work in theater, television and film is literally "behind the scenes." Their efforts are critical to the success of the production. They are the stagehands—a veritable army of technicians who build and set up stages, move and operate the scenery, position props and hang the lighting and sound equipment and run it during the show.

The term stagehand refers to a number of jobs that may differ widely in terms of background required and tasks to be performed. Job titles vary depending on whether the work is in theater, television or motion picture production and on where in the country you're working.

The traditional image of a stagehand is the crew mem-

ENTERTAINMENT

ber who works in theater. Also called stage technicians, these are the electricians, carpenters, property ("props") handlers and riggers (who may work high above the stage to hang lighting and sound equipment and the cables that raise and lower scenery).

Union stagehands in commercial and nonprofit theaters around the country generally have distinct and separate job responsibilities. In non-union locations, their roles are more interchangeable; an electrician may work as a lighting designer one day and do carpentry or props the next.

In film production the behind-the-scenes work is done by grips, best boys and gaffers, among others. In television studios the workers may be called stagehands or grips. In this chapter we will focus on the stagehands who work in live production for theater, concerts and TV.

Most stagehands do not work continuously. Much of theater is seasonal—for example, summer stock—and even a commercial theater house may not have a play or musical booked for every week of the year. Only a few backstage people are permanent employees of a particular theater; the rest are hired by the producers of an incoming show to work only that show.

When bad reviews or other factors force a show to "close," the stagehands (and everyone else) are once again unemployed. Union members go back to making "calls" to their union local for whatever work is coming up; other stagehands let their various contacts know they're available again. Some workers must find other kinds of jobs during these down times, just as many actors who are between roles must pay the bills by waiting tables.

It's been said that actors get the glory, producers get the money, directors get the control and writers get the satisfaction of seeing their words come to life. What do the stagehands get? They get the satisfaction of knowing that, because of their creative efforts, the magic happens every night.

STAGEHAND

What You Need To Know

- ❏ Basic principles of theatrical staging, lighting and sound
- ❏ Understanding of furniture design helpful
- ❏ Scenery construction and painting
- ❏ Basics of television production

Necessary Skills

- ❏ Adeptness with hand and power tools
- ❏ Computer know-how (lighting, sound and motorized scenery are computerized)
- ❏ Ability to read a blueprint and technical drawings
- ❏ Ability to locate props for a show
- ❏ Welding and metallurgy experience helpful

Do You Have What It Takes?

- ❏ Ability to work well as part of a team
- ❏ Strong organization skills and attention to detail
- ❏ Ability to work rapidly and under pressure
- ❏ Promptness, reliability, strong work ethic
- ❏ Flexibility (change is constant)
- ❏ No fear of heights (very important for electricians and riggers who work on ladders and scaffolding)

Physical Requirements

- ❏ Strength (lifting, carrying, pushing and pulling of furniture, equipment and electrical cables is required)
- ❏ Manual dexterity and mechanical aptitude (to use tools and equipment)
- ❏ Agility, good eye-hand coordination (for climbing, balancing on beams and not hammering your thumb instead of the nail)
- ❏ Good hearing (to run sound equipment)
- ❏ Stamina (stagehands can work 16-hour-plus days)

◆ **Getting into the Field**

ENTERTAINMENT

Education

A high school diploma is preferred.

Licenses Required

None. A driver's license is helpful, especially for those who have to locate props. A props person who obtains firearms for a show may need a gun license, even if the gun is rigged for theatrical purposes.

Stagehands who work in commercial theater usually belong to the century-old union IATSE (the International Alliance of Theatrical Stage Employees). Television stagehands in major markets may belong to IATSE or NABET (the National Association of Broadcast Employees and Technicians).

Job Outlook

Competition for jobs: extremely intense

In nonprofit theaters (the majority of professional theaters), funding cuts often affect the number of productions that can be mounted, reducing job openings. The unions accept only a small number of new apprentices each year, and there is often a waiting list of several years before they are considered.

The Ground Floor

Entry-level jobs: "gofer," intern, union apprentice

A first job often means volunteering with a local theater or getting an unpaid internship. Others may earn a small stipend to get their start in summer stock.

On-the-Job Responsibilities

In union theaters and TV studios, stagehands usually perform only one skill per job "call." In non-union situations or in venues such as industrial shows or rock concerts, they may perform several functions as needed.

STAGEHAND

Entry-Level and Experienced Stagehands

- ❏ Erect stages for plays, concerts and other entertainment events in theaters, concert halls, stadiums
- ❏ Hang backdrops and scenery and build set pieces
- ❏ Obtain props from theaters, warehouses, merchants or manufacturers, or build props
- ❏ During performances, arrange props for each scene and change scenery
- ❏ Climb ladders or scaffolding to ceiling gridwork and attach cables or ropes through ceiling grids to raise and lower scenery, curtains, lights, etc.
- ❏ Hang lighting on and around stage areas; position and focus fixtures
- ❏ Connect electrical wiring from fixtures to power sources and control panels
- ❏ Position sound equipment (microphones, speakers, amplifiers) on and around stage areas
- ❏ Operate lighting and sound equipment during rehearsals and performances

◆ When You'll Work

Stagehands often work beyond an eight-hour shift. A 12-hour (or more) day is common, especially when you are bringing in a new theater production or setting up a rock-and-roll concert stage under intense time pressure. During a show's run, working evenings, weekends and holidays is required. Theaters typically offer eight weekly performances, including two or three matinees (afternoon shows).

◆ Time Off

Unless a stagehand has a permanent slot with a theater or TV studio, or is in a union, paid vacation is rare. Most workers are essentially independent contractors who are hired for a single production or time period.

ENTERTAINMENT

Perks
- Opportunity to meet famous performers
- Free or discount tickets to theater or TV productions
- Union stagehands generally get health insurance, paid vacation, sick leave and, at a big local, possibly a pension plan

Who's Hiring
- Commercial legitimate theaters (Broadway, Off Broadway and in big cities)
- Theater production companies
- Regional (nonprofit) theaters all across the U.S.
- University and college theaters
- Dinner theaters
- Touring companies (theaters, rock shows, dance companies and ice shows)
- Television stations (commercial, independent and public stations)
- Corporate industrial shows
- Concert halls, opera houses
- Art and cultural centers
- Summer theaters, outdoor pageants
- Theme parks (Walt Disney World, Opryland, etc.)
- Circuses

Places You'll Go

Beginners and experienced stagehands: occasional travel

When a theater production, usually from Broadway, starts touring the country, a core group of stage technicians who are familiar with the show will travel with it. Such touring companies may be on the road for months.

Surroundings

Backstage there's dust, and an empty theater may be chilly or stuffy. Trucks may be unloaded in unappealing back alleys in the middle of the night or during the day on sidewalks crowded with pedestrians.

On-the-Job Hazards

❏ Hearing damage (from long-term exposure to loud music in enclosed spaces)
❏ Potential for accidents when moving heavy scenery or props
❏ Danger of falling from great heights (for riggers)
❏ Hot lights can cause burns

Dollars and Cents

Wages vary depending on whether the locale is union or non-union, the theater's size, the producer's budget, what region of the country you're working in, and your experience and specific duties. Generally, but not always, union jobs pay more than non-union. Union stagehands in large cities may earn, on average, an hourly rate in the high teens; crew bosses and riggers may earn $25 an hour. On union jobs, overtime ("time and a half") usually kicks in after an eight-hour shift, and double time starts after 16 hours.

Moving Up

Experienced stagehands may become supervisors in their respective areas (e.g., head electrician or carpenter) or, possibly, stage managers. Others may go to work for the manufacturers and suppliers of equipment for sound, light and special effects. In television they may work their way up to a job as technical director for a particular program. In theater, union stagehands often keep doing the same job for decades; seniority allows first choice among available jobs.

Where the Jobs Are

New York City remains the theater capital, but Los Angeles, Chicago, San Francisco and Boston also have an active year-round theater scene. Around the country, the several hundred nonprofit regional theaters provide many jobs in professional theater.

In television production most job opportunities for stagehands remain in Hollywood or New York City, along with some TV stations in the biggest markets.

ENTERTAINMENT

Training

Most stagehands learn on the job by observing more experienced colleagues. Many community and junior colleges offer theater-related associate degrees.

The Male/Female Equation

Of the 75,000 members of IATSE, the majority are male. In non-union situations, women may find it easier to get jobs.

Making Your Decision: What to Consider

The Bad News

❏ Long hours are the norm
❏ Night and weekend work is common
❏ Pay is relatively low, especially at the start
❏ Regular periods of unemployment are common

The Good News

❏ Opportunity to work in an exciting, creative field
❏ Casual dress on the job
❏ Often great camaraderie among the crew, especially on tour
❏ Freedom from nine-to-five work

WHAT IT'S REALLY LIKE

Sean Walsh, 25,
stagehand, Shubert Theatre,
Chicago, Illinois
Years in the field: two

How did you break into this business?
My father has been a stagehand with Local 2 (IATSE) for 30 years. In high school I helped out part time. After spending four years in the Navy, I went in front of the (union) executive board and started calling for the extra jobs.

What is your current position?
I'm the full-time union apprentice in the electrical department at the Shubert Theatre. I'm assistant to the house electrician, who does everything from running an extension cord to lighting the show. I also do odds and ends for the house carpenter.

What's a typical day like at the Shubert?
If a show's coming in, I help set it up, which usually takes a few days. When the show starts, the props apprentice and I mop the floor before the show and stand by and watch

everybody else's cues (for changes in lighting, scenery, etc.). We're like understudies—we have to know all the cues if we ever have to fill in for the regular crew. If we do, we're paid journeyman (regular) scale. As an apprentice I'm paid roughly 45 percent of what a journeyman gets.

What other work do you do?
When the Shubert isn't booked, I call the union every day at 3 P.M. They might say, "Go to the circus at Chicago Stadium 6:30 tomorrow night and run a follow spot" (literally the spotlight that follows a performer). Usually they say, "Call back tomorrow." The journeymen all have to be working before I get a job.

I really like to do rock-and-roll shows. I ran follow spot for Bon Jovi, and I've also worked shows for the Grateful Dead, Jethro Tull, Peter Gabriel, U2 and Aerosmith.

After eight hours we get time and a half, and after 16 hours it's all double time. We once worked 37 hours straight to tear down the stage. You practically get a month's pay for working a week, but you *feel* like you've worked a month!

Is physical strength important in this work?
Yes. There is a lot of pulling cable and hauling equipment. I'm 6'4" and about 240 pounds, so the guys love to see me because they know they won't have to pull as hard!

What do you like most about being a stagehand?
I really enjoy the theater and the rock shows. I've met stars like Ann-Margret and Phil Collins.

What's the down side of the job?
The unpredictability of whether or not you'll be working. You'll have two weeks of no work and no pay, and next month you'll have made a thousand dollars. Also, it's rough trying to date. My last girlfriend and I broke up because she was working nine to five and I was often busy working nights.

Charles S. Brightly Jr., 32,
freelance stage technician,
Cartersville, Georgia
Years in the business: five

How did you get into this field?
I was studying to be a chiropractor, but I finally realized that it wasn't for me. I'd always been interested in music and in concert production. I started an 18-month music and video business program at the Art Institute of Atlanta. I found out I just didn't have the "ear" to be a recording engineer, but I did have a really good eye for video and a knack for stage work.

When did you become a stagehand?
Some friends who were doing concert security in Atlanta started asking me to help out—I'm 6'2" and weigh 235. I did more and more of that. Then I talked to the guy who ran a local crew about trying to become a stagehand. He asked what I could do. I said that I was learning concert production and that I used to work for a heavy equipment company. He needed a forklift driver to help build the stage for a George Michael concert at Fulton County Stadium, so I did that and it worked out fine. So he said, "Let's see what you can do as a stagehand." It was just being at the right place at the right time.

What are your job responsibilities?
Building sets and scenery, hanging lights and sound equipment, hooking up speakers, running the correct cables to correct places. You have to pay attention and pick it up mostly on the job. I learned the basics at school, but out in the "real world" there are time pressures. You may have to unload 6 or 12 truckloads of gear and set up a concert in less than 12 hours, so you really have to work fast and safe.

What is your current position?
I'm an independent contractor and work primarily with two companies, Production Arts Workshop and Crew One. They specialize in technicians for concerts and industrial (corporate) shows. These companies bid on acts that come to town, and when they get the job, they call techs like me to ask if we're available. On rock-and-roll shows, I'm usu-

ENTERTAINMENT

ally a carpenter and also spend a lot of time running spotlight. Nine dollars per hour straight time is about the norm (non-union) for concerts around here. On industrials, which pay much better, I do a lot of audiovisual, which includes anything from setting up screens and A/V projectors to running camera.

Have you been a "roadie" on tour with a band?
Not on tour, actually, but a few times I've gone to other cities. I worked the (Paul) McCartney show in Atlanta and Charlotte. We worked 16-hour days to get that show up and ready to go.

What do you like most about your work?
I don't feel like I'm going to a job. I really like the people I work with; the money is good. I get to do different things, which keeps it fresh. Recently I finally got to work with the up-riggers—I hung 130 feet in the air at the Omni. They saw that I was real safe on the ground and concerned with what's going on. Up-rigging is high-dollar work—$20 to $22 an hour—because it's dangerous.

I love sitting back and taking a look at the final product—whether it's a concert stage or a video—and saying, "Dang, that looks good!" I like the different companies and tours that come in town. I was the cameraman for Luther Vandross's shows in Atlanta, which was part of the stagehand work (the image magnification on large screens during the concert). I did an industrial show that brought in the Temptations and the Four Tops. And I've had lunch with Paul McCartney!

What do you like least about the work?
I don't like being away from my wife and five-year-old son, and sometimes that happens. We live almost 50 miles from Atlanta. If I'm working two or three shows there, that can mean staying there for a week and not going home.

What advice would you give someone considering this career?
You have to have a positive attitude, jump in, work hard, and be willing to try to do anything. Don't say "All I want to do is lights"—be willing to do carpentry or sound or work on the set. You have to communicate well with the client, your supervisor and the other people you work with.

Getting along well with everyone is essential and shows professionalism.

Marilyn Maes, 37, stage technician, ABC-TV, Hollywood, California
Years in the field: 17

What is your current position?
I run the warehouse for *General Hospital* (a soap opera). I take care of all the props, furniture, carpets and linoleum. I'm full-time staff with ABC. If I didn't have this position I would be "bouncing" with the union (IATSE).

How did you break into the business?
When I was 17, I moved to Los Angeles from my home in New Mexico. I was giving shampoos at a hair salon, and a customer told me I had strong hands. He said he worked for CBS-TV and he thought I'd make a great stagehand. When he asked me what I'd done before, I told him I'd worked at a leather company sewing wallets on industrial sewing machines. He said I could probably work in the CBS drapery department.

He gave me a tour of CBS, and I went to talk to the man in drapery. He said, "I don't have time to talk with you unless you can fix this sewing machine!" The thread kept breaking on him. It was the same machine I'd worked on before, so I said, "No problem." I fixed it and he hired me!

I was just thrilled to be working on TV, walking on the set of Carol Burnett's show. I stayed in drapery six months, but there wasn't enough work for full time, so I started bouncing. I'd call the union and get work wherever they sent me. I'd do props, electric, grip work, even cleaning.

How did you learn all those jobs?
On-the-job training. The union used to send new people over to NBC. They taught you how to work with other people and to work safely, to wear your hard boots, to always carry your tools on you.

ENTERTAINMENT

I wasn't unfamiliar with tools because I'd learned from my father, who'd been a construction foreman. I'd always paid attention to how he held the nail and how he handled tools. My dream was to work construction with my dad, but he passed away before I was old enough to be on my own.

After about five years of bouncing, I began working steadily at the *General Hospital* warehouse. For two years I worked the props. I sometimes worked 17 hours a day. At that time the stagehands also did all the cooking for food used on the show. Now they send out for it.

What's a typical day in your current job?
I come in at 6 A.M. and check with the crew that set up the stage during the night for today's taping. They often tell me the director made a change—he struck one set and they need another. So I'm there to get that set to the stage before they start blocking tape (marking the set for the actors' movements) at 8:30 A.M.

Then I go to the warehouse (on the other side of the studio lot) and meet my other crew. I have four steady crew members, and I also get four extra people from the local every day. We pull the sets needed for the next day out of the warehouse and take them to the stage. Then we take the sets they used yesterday and store them in the warehouse. The sets we use regularly are always in the warehouse. Less frequently used sets are rented, and I make sure they get sent back to the rental companies.

I usually leave at 6 P.M. The night crew comes in at 9 P.M. to strike the stage when taping is over and to put in the next show. They should be done by 7:30 or 8 the next morning. By that time I'm already back.

How important is physical strength on this job?
Very important. You've got to keep up your health and eat right. You also have to do things the proper way. I'm 5'5" and 130 pounds, and I can lift as much as any other person, maybe more, because I follow the basics, like how to bend your legs and handle the item with both hands instead of one.

Safety is very important. A lot of workers like to take my "call" because they say I'm very safe and cautious. I don't let them unload a truck until everyone and everything is ready.

What do you like most about this work?
Working outside a lot. I'm able to open up the big doors and greet the sun or rain or cold. I get to wear Levi's and tennis shoes to work. I handle beautiful furniture. I enjoy seeing movie stars and working with different people every day.

I'm very proud of the warehouse. People enjoy coming to work at a place that's clean. I learned that from my dad. He always cleaned up after himself and left things neat and ready for the next day, and I believe in that.

What do you like least about the work?
The long hours.

What advice would you give aspiring stagehands?
Pay attention. It's so helpful when someone really listens to you and does the job the way you ask. Common sense is so very important, and it isn't so common.

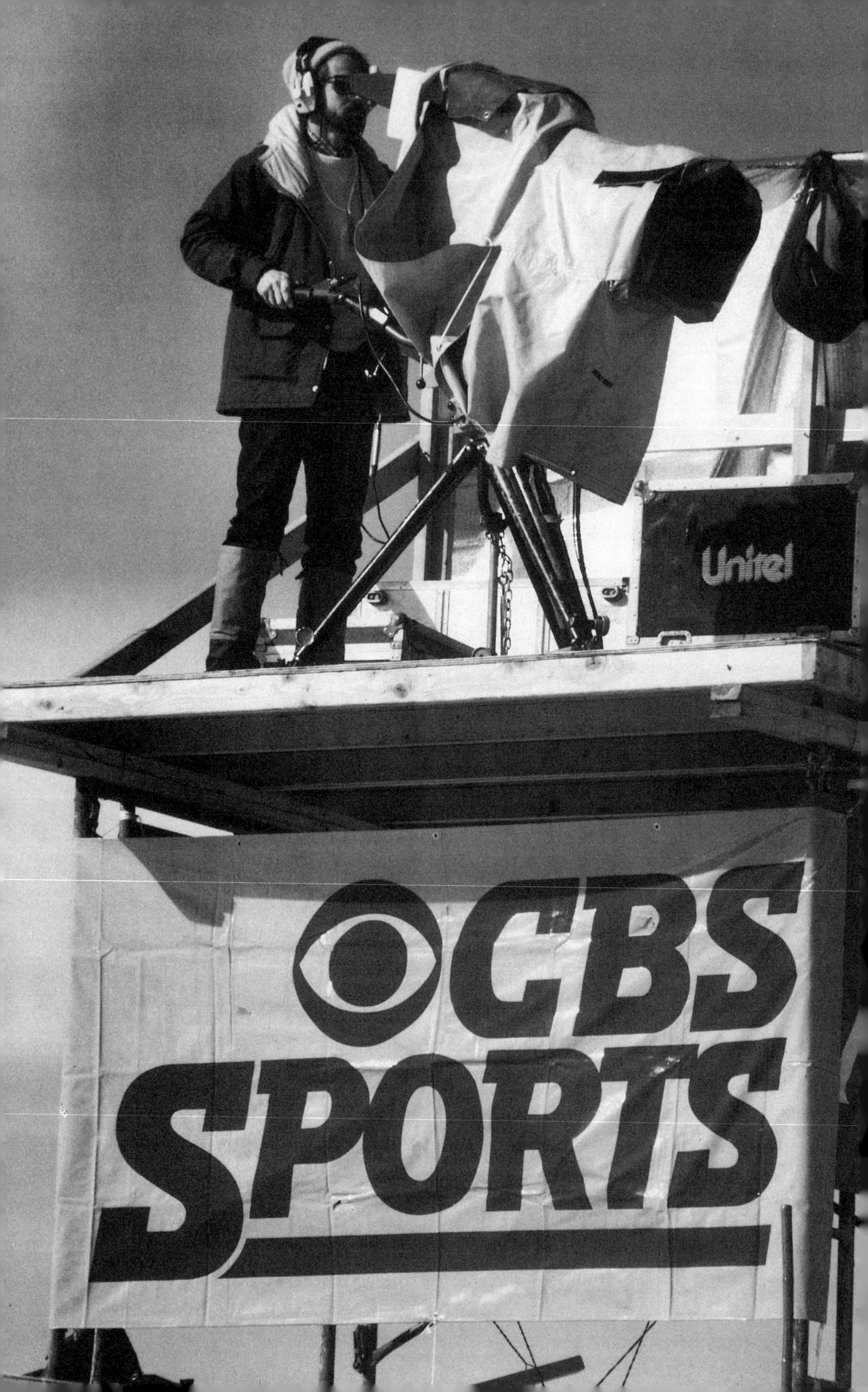

Unitel
CBS
SPORTS

CAMERA OPERATOR

You're in a movie theater, watching the credits begin to roll. You notice one or more names listed as "camera operator." You've always been a camera buff; you think, What a fun and exciting job it must be! You're right. But there's a great deal more to this demanding career than simply keeping a performer in focus—you have to understand lighting, lenses, film type and more.

Camera operators are responsible for the actual physical operation of a film or video camera. In a television studio or in film production, that may be a several hundred pound camera (called a "hard" camera) mounted on a pedestal or movable platform. Or it could be a small, shoulder-rest "mini-cam" (about 40 pounds), commonly used in TV electronic

ENTERTAINMENT

news gathering ("ENG") or for shooting remote segments for entertainment programs.

In television, video cameras are used to shoot such programs as soap operas, game and talk shows and children's and newsmagazine shows. Most prime-time dramas and many sitcoms are shot in film, which gives a higher image quality than videotape. All major motion pictures are shot in 35-millimeter film; small-budget films, generally in 16-millimeter.

Making a motion picture is a team effort, and operating the camera is both a technical and creative process. The movie's director tells the director of photography (the "DP") what effect or mood he desires in a scene, and the DP communicates this to the camera operator. Scenes can range from a wide-angle spectacle featuring the proverbial cast of thousands to an intimate, candlelit close-up of two people. In small productions the DP may also operate the camera, but in major films there is always a separate camera operator.

Beginning camera operators often get a start with a small independent film or documentary, in which a film crew may consist of as few as four people and everyone wears several hats. Others begin in corporate or industrial production, such as a company's educational or training films. On a major feature film, an aspiring camera operator never starts behind the camera. More often, the first job is as a film loader or a second assistant camera person.

In television, an entry-level job may be as a "vacation relief" or "utility" person. Typical functions include helping the camera operator move the equipment around the studio and helping the audio person set up a boom microphone or "mike" the talent or guests.

Most jobs are freelance and are rarely, if ever, advertised, so you need a web of contacts to stay employed. But this is still very much a field in which you really learn the ropes on the job rather than in the classroom, and there's always a chance to stand out and shine.

CAMERA OPERATOR

◆ Getting into the Field

What You Need to Know

- ❏ Basics of television, film and video production processes
- ❏ Basic camera angles and placements
- ❏ Basic film lighting techniques
- ❏ Math, physics and chemistry (to understand the workings of lenses, film speed, light sources)
- ❏ Principles of composition and perspective (such as how to create a sense of depth on a flat plane)

Necessary Skills

- ❏ Good communication (you must understand what the DP or the client wants)
- ❏ An "eye" for framing pictures—artistic sense
- ❏ Ability to fix equipment on location
- ❏ Attention to detail

Do You Have What It Takes?

- ❏ Ability to work under time pressure
- ❏ Ability to work as part of a team
- ❏ Patience (especially in film production, where much time is spent waiting for crews to set up)
- ❏ Business sense (camera operators are often freelancers)
- ❏ A strong work ethic

Physical Requirements

- ❏ Strength and stamina to move cameras or carry minicams and accessories, possibly for hours
- ❏ Manual dexterity—"nimble fingers" (to manipulate equipment, load film magazines quickly, etc.)
- ❏ Fast reflexes

ENTERTAINMENT

Education

A high school diploma is generally required. Coursework in film or video production is helpful, but practical experience is more valued than classes in film theory.

Licenses Required

None. At the television networks, camera operators must belong to a union, either NABET (the National Association of Broadcast Engineers and Technicians) or IBEW (the International Brotherhood of Electrical Workers). Commercial TV stations in large markets also tend to be unionized. Some TV camera people and most camera operators on major motion pictures belong to IATSE (the International Alliance of Theatrical Stage Employees and Moving Picture Machine Operators of the U.S. and Canada).

Job Outlook

Competition for jobs: extremely intense

All the TV networks and large TV stations have been downsizing in recent years to cut costs, which means job openings are fewer. However, greater job growth is expected in cable television and independent video production.

The Ground Floor

Entry-level jobs: film loader, second assistant camera person (film); production assistant (film or TV)

In major feature films, the camera operator is aided by the first and second assistant camera persons. The first assistant (or sometimes the second) is also called the focus puller, because during shooting he or she sits with the camera operator and makes sure the lens is in focus for every scene and changes lenses and filters as needed.

The second assistant camera person helps the first assistant in all duties. He or she also operates the slate and clapstick to mark each "take" of a scene before shooting begins and usually is responsible for shipping exposed film to the lab for processing at the end of each day. The film loader is responsible for loading and unloading the film magazines (the lightproof containers that hold the film) in the camera.

In TV or film, the production assistant ("PA") does all manner of "gofer" tasks to help smooth the film process. For example, when a movie is being filmed on a city street, a PA may be stationed at the end of the block to prevent the public from walking into a scene during filming.

Film Camera Operators

- ❏ Look through the camera and guide it as the action of a scene occurs, obtaining the image the director wants
- ❏ Frame each scene according to precise instructions from the DP regarding setup, angles, distances and other variables
- ❏ Direct the dolly grip on camera movements (the dolly is a wheeled platform holding the camera, allowing smooth movements during a scene)
- ❏ Direct the first and second assistants on various tasks

TV Camera Operators

- ❏ In the TV studio during a shooting, follow camera angle directions received through headphones from the director or technical director
- ❏ Assist in the setup and maintenance of TV cameras
- ❏ May help the lighting director set up lighting equipment
- ❏ May do "set dressing," such as arranging tabletop items or chairs for attractive framing of the scene

◆ **On-the-Job Responsibilities**

ENTERTAINMENT

When You'll Work

In prime time television, particularly when working on hour-long dramas, 12- to 16-hour days can be the norm. In major film production, 14- or 15-hour days are also routine, and camera setup may begin before dawn. Principal photography (the actual shooting of the film) generally takes from three to five months.

Time Off

Union camera operators on staff with a television station, network or production company get paid vacation, usually after six months. Those who are not on staff ("per diem" hires) are essentially independent contractors who choose their own—unpaid—vacation time.

Perks

- Opportunity to meet and work with famous actors or musicians (in features or music videos)
- Chance that your work will be seen nationally or even internationally
- Health insurance, paid vacation, retirement benefits with union position

Who's Hiring

- Film and video production companies
- Commercial and public television stations
- Television networks
- Cable TV networks (ESPN, USA, MTV, etc.)
- Local cable systems
- Advertising agencies (for commercials)
- Corporate audiovisual (A-V) departments (for training and educational films and video)

Places You'll Go

Motion picture camera operators often travel to varied and exotic locales during several months of shooting. Camera operators for independent video production companies also travel a great deal of the time, though on much shorter schedules—perhaps three days crammed with shooting to produce a 15-minute TV segment. Television camera operators are more likely to work on the same set each day. Some TV programs, especially network news/entertainment shows, often do remotes around the country.

Surroundings

Film and video camera operators may work in a controlled studio setting or outdoors on location in a wide variety of environments. Television employees may spend most of their time in a modern, air-conditioned studio. If they do a remote, they may travel in the station's equipment-filled mobile van to locales ranging from a celebrity's beautiful home to a bleak industrial neighborhood.

Dollars and Cents

In television, network jobs pay the best. Network-affiliated TV stations pay more than independent stations. Similarly, stations in the biggest markets pay higher salaries than smaller markets, and commercial stations pay more than public (noncommercial) stations. Union camera operators at the networks and large TV stations earn more than workers at non-union stations. Cable is more likely to be non-union. An entry-level union camera operator may earn $500 a week or more in a major market or less than $300 a week in a small market. A camera operator at the network level may get $350 a day or more. In films, the minimum day rate for a union camera operator is about $35 per hour plus benefits. Experienced camera operators can earn $1,200 a day or more.

Moving Up

A television camera operator may move up to be a lighting director, a technical director or engineering supervisor, or the director of photography for a particular program. Others may move up to network news or documentary units where they have more independence and where greater judgment and creativity are required. Some specialize in shooting TV commercials, which can be highly lucrative.

Motion picture camera operators generally want to become directors of photography. It takes years to build a reputation and be considered a "cinematographer," which

ENTERTAINMENT

usually happens by way of an invitation to join the prestigious professional group, the American Society of Cinematographers.

Where the Jobs Are

Most jobs for television camera operators are at the 1,150 commercial stations in the U.S.; there are also 365 noncommercial TV stations. In addition to the broadcast television network headquarters in New York City, network operations are in Los Angeles, San Francisco, Chicago and Washington D.C. and in bureaus in cities such as Miami and Atlanta. There are nearly 11,000 cable TV stations across the country, but not all do original production (that requires camera operators).

Motion picture production is still concentrated in Los Angeles and New York, though work is increasing in Nashville, Chicago, San Francisco, Dallas, Houston, Orlando, Miami, Atlanta and Pittsburgh. There is also a lot of U.S. production in Toronto and Vancouver, Canada. There are hundreds of independent film and video production companies, most of which are based in New York and Los Angeles.

Training

Camera operators generally learn on the job. Some technical or broadcast training can be obtained at many community colleges or specialty film/video production schools. The American Film Institute conducts regular workshops and seminars in major cities around the country on various aspects of filmmaking. For information and brochures, write AFI, Public Service Programs, P.O. Box 27999, 2021 North Western Avenue, Los Angeles, California 90027.

The Male/Female Equation

Most camera operators are male. In the large Los Angeles IATSE camera local, just over 10 percent of the 3,500 members are women. Opportunities for women are increasing, though, especially in cable and public TV.

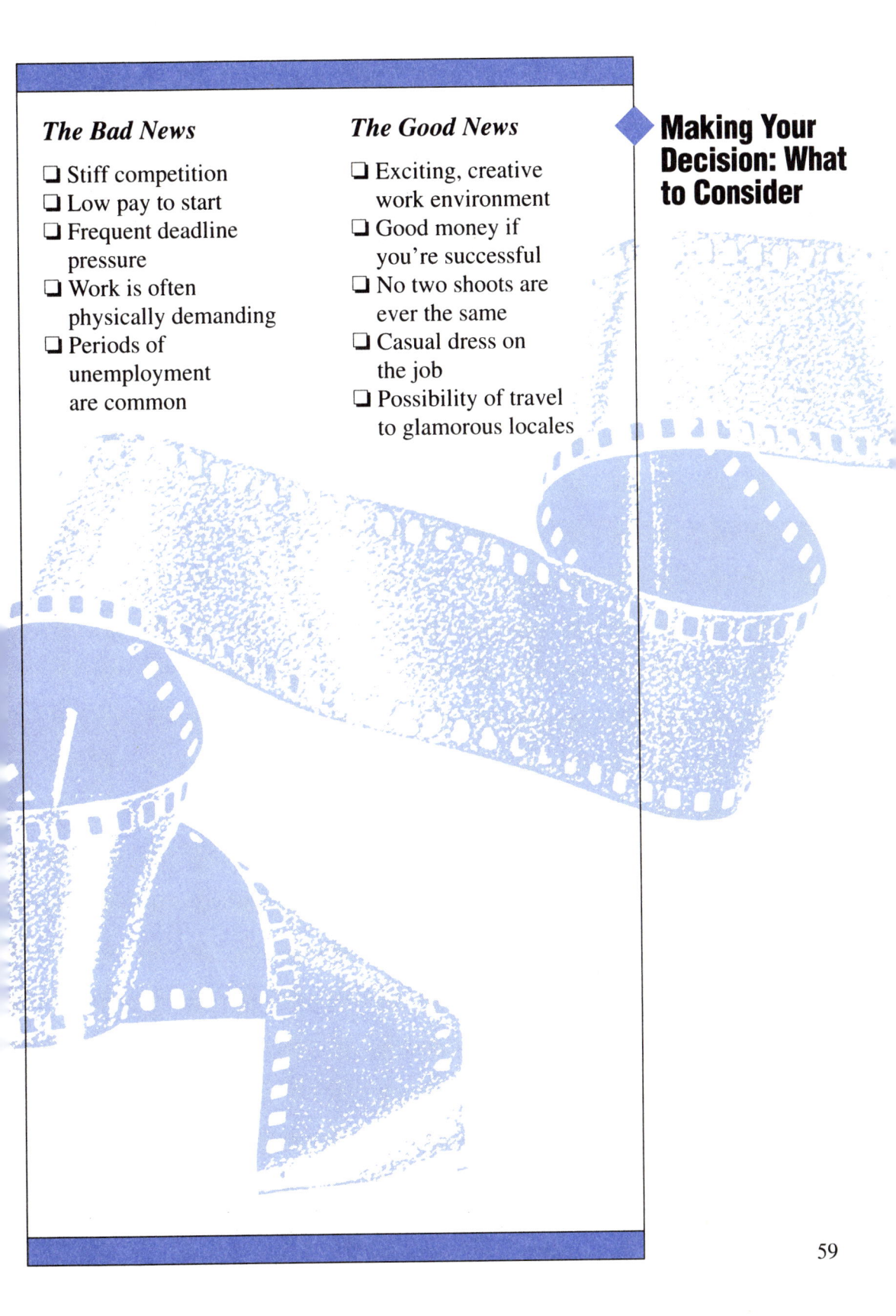

CAMERA OPERATOR

◆ Making Your Decision: What to Consider

The Bad News
- Stiff competition
- Low pay to start
- Frequent deadline pressure
- Work is often physically demanding
- Periods of unemployment are common

The Good News
- Exciting, creative work environment
- Good money if you're successful
- No two shoots are ever the same
- Casual dress on the job
- Possibility of travel to glamorous locales

ENTERTAINMENT

WHAT IT'S REALLY LIKE

Gary Nardilla, 32,
director of photography,
Citicam Productions,
New York, New York
Years in the field: 12

What is your current position?
I have been a director of photography with my own production company since 1985. Among other jobs, we shoot network and syndicated entertainment and newsmagazine shows. We've done work for *Entertainment Tonight,* HBO, Showtime, MTV and *Lifestyles of the Rich and Famous.* Most jobs are video, but some are film.

How did you get into this business?
After high school I became a bicycle messenger for a division of Columbia Pictures. I picked up packages from the studios and watched what was going on. I wanted to be a part of it, so I went to a TV trade school at night for about ten months. I learned the basic lingo and production process. After getting my certificate, I got hired as a vacation relief in the WOR-TV newsroom. I started out doing audio with the field crews.

CAMERA OPERATOR

When did you get to operate a camera?
After five months as vacation relief they put me on staff, and they let me start training on cameras in my spare time. After about a year, when news was breaking and the regular cameramen were already out, the news director would say, "Nardilla, grab a camera and get out there and do it!"

What other camera jobs have you had?
I was with WOR for two and a half years, then I got hired at the New York office of *Entertainment Tonight*. I learned a lot more about shooting; ET was two steps above news in quality. They might spend an hour lighting an interview setting nicely. Right from the start my job sheet was non-stop celebrities. At 9 A.M. it might be Charles Bronson; at 3 P.M., Raquel Welch; the next day, Luciano Pavarotti.

Do you still go out and do shoots now?
Unlike DPs on major features, I'm still behind the camera. I mainly do the higher-level production jobs, the kind that are very lighting intensive, and larger on-location film jobs that require multiple grip trucks. There's much more calculation in lighting film. You have to know film stock and lenses; you have to know what contrast ratio you can get away with on this particular film stock and lighting setup. You have to know how fast or slow you want the film to be and what kind of effect you want to create in the scene.

What do you like most about your work?
It allows you and your team to create something that didn't exist before. And there's the satisfaction of knowing that your hard work and effort shows. People say, "I saw that special last night that you did, and it looked great!"

What do you like least?
Being away from my family. This business often takes you away on extended trips. My work has taken me to 30 countries. It can be very glamorous and exciting, but the shoots can be very hard.

What advice would you give aspiring camera operators?
So many people want to get in that the point is, are you going to shine compared to the person next to you? You have to set your mind to what you want and say, Even if I'm a P.A. I'm going to be the best P.A. they remember.

ENTERTAINMENT

Even if you're just bringing coffee, do it better than everybody else. If you do, people will start relying on you. The more they see you can handle, the more responsibility they'll keep giving you.

Annie McEveety, 34,
first assistant camera person, Los Angeles, California
Years in the field: 13

What is your current position?
I've been a first assistant camera person (first AC) for six years; I was a second assistant for seven years before that. I've worked on many feature films, television shows and commercials. I prefer features.

How did you get into this business?
After high school I got a job in the mailroom of Disney Studios in Burbank. Whenever I could, I'd go observe at the animation sets. After four months on the job, several of us from the mailroom were brought into the animation camera department to do on-the-job training on "TRON." It got me into the same union as the live-action camera people. I spent four years in animation getting my seniority, then I bugged camera people until I got my first job in live action in 1981.

What was hardest at first about being in live action?
The overwhelming sense of responsibility. If you white light a roll of used film (ruin it by exposing it to light), the entire day's work could be on it—and maybe it was a $500,000 day. They'd have to call everybody back and reshoot it because of *you*. In this business, if you screw up you very seldom get a second chance.

What's involved in being a first AC?
I build the camera every day and pull focus for the camera operator during filming. I'm responsible for all the cameras, equipment, film and lenses. The day before each shoot I get the "call sheet" outlining the shooting schedule and make sure I have everything we'll need for every

CAMERA OPERATOR

scene. I also do all the camera maintenance. I stayed a second AC a long time so that when I became a first AC I'd know exactly what I was doing. The first AC, camera operator and dolly grip all have to think alike—it's like a well-oiled machine.

How did you get jobs when you started out?
Persistence. I called people *all* the time and begged for work. The cameraman who hired me for my second job did so after I told him he could fire me after a day if he didn't want me. That's how you've got to be at the start. It's only been in the last few years that I haven't had to hunt down work.

Is physical strength important in your job?
Yes. The camera assists have to carry the camera and equipment. I'm five feet three inches and weigh 119 pounds. The camera on the tripod weighs about 115 pounds. But once you learn balance it feels like only 40 pounds. I didn't move up to first AC until I learned to carry that camera anywhere.

Do you want to become a camera operator?
Yes, but not until I know there are at least four cameramen who will give me work. Before I moved up to first AC, I made sure that four cameramen would hire me.

What do you like most about your job?
The responsibility. I've *done* something, and I feel good at the end of the day. You meet so many creative people. Sometimes I think, Wow, I get *paid* for this?

What do you like least?
The hours. A typical day is at least 12 hours—7 A.M. to 7 P.M., with a half-hour lunch. Occasionally you have to work seven days, but then I make double time, which could mean $106 an hour.

What advice would you give an aspiring camera person?
Get on a film as an extra. It's non-union, and you can observe on the set. Get to know who the camera people are, and they'll get to know you. If you keep coming around, it's inevitable that there's going to be a time when they'll need someone to help them. If you're there to offer

63

ENTERTAINMENT

your services for free, eventually somebody's going to give you a (paying) job.

The way you go places in this business is by reputation. You don't want to be late, you don't want to complain, you want to be on set all the time, and then you want to do a good job.

The key to being in camera is anticipation. You learn to read minds and know what people want before they ask for it; you have to be aware of what's going on around you. If you have that and ambition, I can't see you not succeeding.

Charles T. Henry, 36,
electronic camera operator,
ABC Television Network,
Hollywood, California
Years in the field: 15

What is your current position?
I'm the West Coast camera operator for *Good Morning America*. The audio person and I—we're a team—travel anywhere west of the Mississippi.

How did you break into this business?
When I got out of high school I was a mail clerk for WABC-TV in New York City. One day I applied for and got an internship with the station's *Eyewitness News*. After six months I became a TelePrompTer operator on the news set. Later I got to work on the new video cameras. They saw I was a quick learner, and they hired me as a camera operator for *Eyewitness News*.

What sort of training or background did you have?
I was a self-taught photographer; I took wedding photos while I was in high school. I was pretty adept at the framing, composition and lighting. I developed my own black-and-whites in a home darkroom. As a camera operator, I learned everything on the job. After about a year I transferred to ABC network sports. I went around the country doing college football, car races, great stuff.

CAMERA OPERATOR

What was hardest at first about shooting in the field for sports rather than in a studio?
Making sure the camera worked. It came in boxes; you literally had to put it together like a puzzle. It was so big and heavy that it would take four guys to pick up the camera body—without the lens—and put it on the pedestal. Now one person can do it, but you still need two people for the lens.

The technology keeps changing drastically on video cameras. There's a lot more electronics inside them now, which means there's less to do. When I started out, I had to do all the registration (focusing, etc.) myself. Now I just put the camera on a pedestal, push a button and the computer does it.

What other camera operator work have you done?
I worked on all of the New York ABC soap operas for about five years. Then I went back into local news for a year and worked as an ENG camera operator out in the field, working off the truck and microwaving stuff around. It helped prepare me for coming to Los Angeles in 1986. I worked camera for *General Hospital* for two years. Then I became a floater—I shot sitcoms, game shows, sports and newsmagazine programs. I floated for two years, then went back to *General Hospital* until I joined *Good Morning America*.

What's a typical day like?
At about 6 A.M. I pick up the (equipment) truck at the Hollywood studio. Usually we'll be getting ready to go to a celebrity interview, either at their hotel or their home. We may spend a day shooting the interview. Usually we get done around 6 P.M. We average 12 hours a day.

What do you like most about your work?
What I'm doing right now gives me a little more control. In certain cases I can pretty much become my own director and set designer. The producers have an idea of what they want, but they depend on me heavily to give them a great shot.

What do you like least about the work?
I miss my wife and three-year-old daughter. It's a lot of travel, and I'm on call 24 hours a day. I don't spend

ENTERTAINMENT

enough time in a particular location to have my family join me.

What achievement are you most proud of so far?
I want to get an individual Emmy for my own camera work, and this job will give me the chance to hopefully hit that mark. I've received three group Emmys (for a team effort). I got my first for technical excellence in electronic camera on *One Life to Live*, a second for the 1984 Los Angeles Olympics, and a third for the 1988 Calgary Olympics. Actually, my greatest achievement was meeting my wife at the 1984 Olympics!

What advice would you give aspiring camera operators?
Because of the downsizing going on at all the networks, I'd encourage people to get to know the cable companies. They are carrying more and more original programming, and with the advent of 500 cable channels they're going to need the bodies.

CAMERA OPERATOR

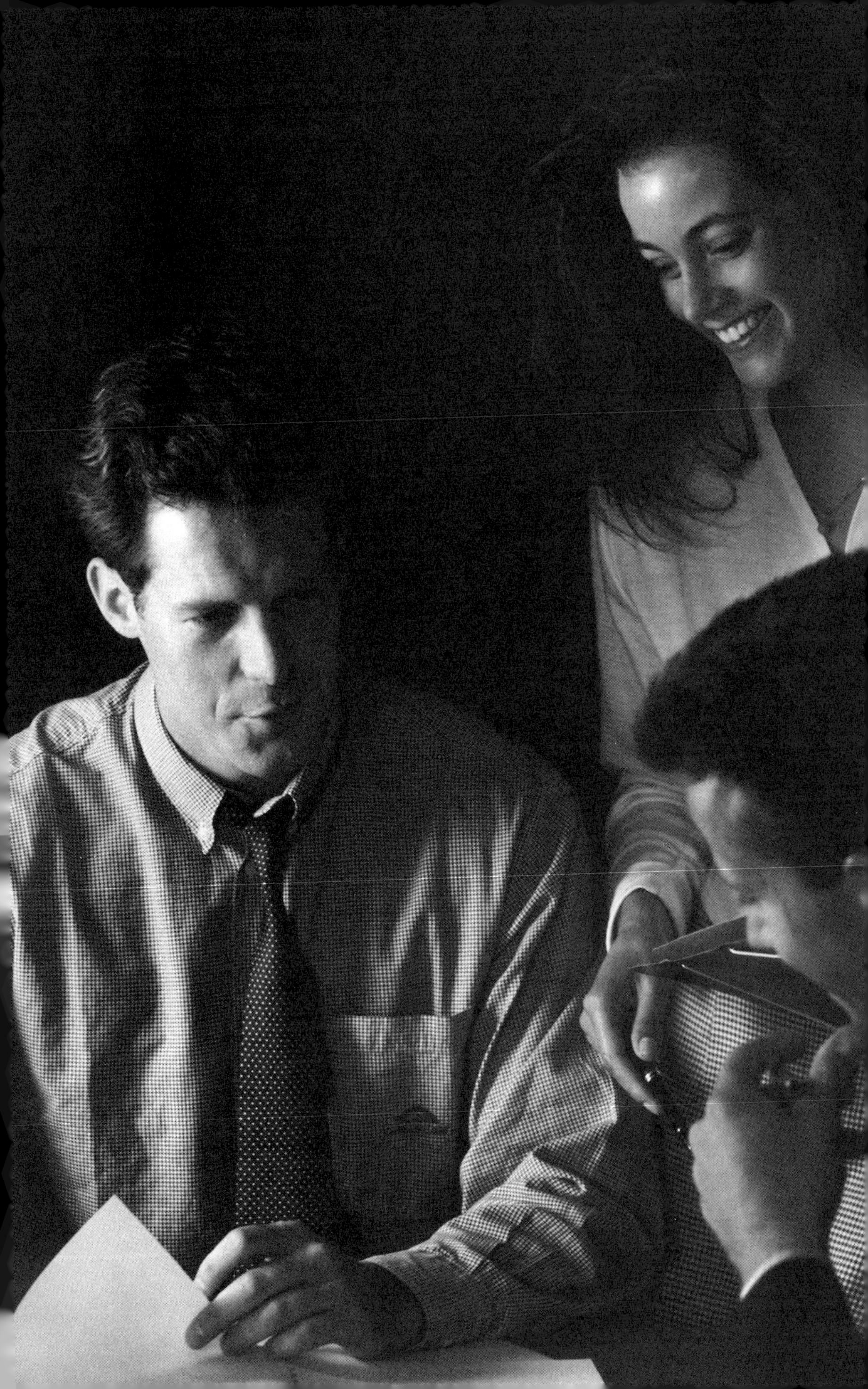

TIME SALESPERSON

The people who sell television or radio commercials are vitally important to their respective stations because the revenues from advertising literally keep the stations on the air. To sell time successfully, the salesperson must be familiar with all the station's programming, ratings and audience demographics—which shows are targeted to, say, women under 24 or men over 45.

Broadcast time salespeople (also called account executives or sales representatives) have a special challenge because what they sell is intangible: The prospective buyer can't kick the tires or try on the clothes. Sales reps have to convince potential clients of the advertising value of their medium (radio, TV or cable) to the client's business and also con-

ENTERTAINMENT

vince them of the cost-effective benefits of their particular station. Then, by analyzing the client's product or service and the customers they want to attract, sales reps devise an ad program to achieve the desired results.

Radio and TV reps sell commercials only on their station, but the cable sales rep needs to know which of the many ad-supported cable networks on a particular cable system is the best place for a client's message.

Time sales can be made at the local, regional or network level. Local and regional sales reps sell "spots," which are commercials that do not air on the networks. Commercials generally are 10, 30 or 60 seconds long and may cost a few or many thousands of dollars.

Unlike their colleagues in print media, broadcasters cannot simply "add a page" when the need for advertising space is higher than expected. When the program is sold out, it's sold out. Thus the sales rep is often working under deadline pressure to try to accommodate a client who makes a late request for advertising time.

A first job in time sales is almost always at the local level in a small radio or TV market. Having had some kind of previous sales experience can help, even if you were just selling ads for the high school yearbook. New reps are generally paid a low base salary until they start to build a client list and earn commissions (a percentage of the money they bring in from commercial sales). After six months or so on the job, most sales reps are paid on straight commission. The more they sell, the more they earn.

Getting new clients is not a sales rep's primary goal, but *keeping* them is. A rep needs to maintain regular contact with clients to see that their ad schedule is meeting their needs. The rep also must stay informed about *all* the competition—other radio, TV or cable stations, newspapers, magazines and direct mailers—going after his or her clients.

For those with people skills and competitive drive, selling time in the exciting world of electronic media can be satisfying—and it can be a way to earn big bucks.

TIME SALESPERSON

What You Need to Know

- ❏ Computers (almost all station and research data is computerized)
- ❏ Basic strategies for advertising sales
- ❏ Audience measurement ratings systems (i.e., Arbitron in radio, Nielsen in TV and cable)
- ❏ Basics of research methodology and analysis
- ❏ Familiarity with commercial production techniques helpful
- ❏ General consumer buying trends
- ❏ Strengths of your medium (radio, TV, cable)

Necessary Skills

- ❏ Excellent writing ability (for client presentations and possibly advertising copy)
- ❏ Ability to make a strong "sales pitch"
- ❏ Good listening skills
- ❏ Ability to analyze charts, graphs, research data

Do You Have What It Takes?

- ❏ Guts to ask for the client's order
- ❏ A positive attitude and self-confidence
- ❏ A friendly, outgoing personality
- ❏ Persuasiveness and persistence
- ❏ Ability to work with all types of people
- ❏ Ability to deal with rejection
- ❏ Good organization skills and attention to detail
- ❏ A neat, pleasant appearance; good manners
- ❏ Reliability (you must never forget an appointment)
- ❏ An even temperament—ability to "roll with the punches"

Education

A high school diploma is required.

◆ Getting into the Field

ENTERTAINMENT

Licenses Required

None

Job Outlook

Competition for jobs: very intense

Job openings at radio and TV stations are not expected to increase this decade. However, cable TV is expected to continue its steady—and in some areas, explosive—growth. Many openings come through job turnover.

The Ground Floor

Entry-level job: salesperson or sales assistant

On-the-Job Responsibilities

Time Salespeople

❑ Telephone or visit prospective advertisers to promote the salesperson's station as an advertising medium
❑ Ask prospective clients questions to identify their marketing needs and goals
❑ Consult market research and audience demographics to select the most suitable ad environment for a client
❑ Develop an advertising program to meet those needs; "sell" the client on its value
❑ May assist in the writing and production of a client's commercial
❑ Make sure the client's commercial is produced the way the client wants it and that it airs at the expected times
❑ Regularly monitor client's ad program and handle changes
❑ Entertain clients (at sports events, restaurants, etc.)
❑ Attend meetings regularly to brainstorm marketing ideas

TIME SALESPERSON

When You'll Work

Sales is not a nine-to-five job. Reps often work irregular hours, meeting with clients early in the morning or late at night if that's most convenient for the client. Many reps also do paperwork on weekends or go into the office to handle a problem. Reps also spend some of their own time watching or listening to competitors' programming and noting who their advertisers are.

Time Off

A week's vacation is generally available after six months on the job and possibly sooner. Major holidays are generally observed and the sales department is officially closed.

Perks

- Free tickets to concerts or sports events involving the station or its advertisers
- Free merchandise related to advertisers or networks
- Liberal expense account for entertaining clients

Who's Hiring

- Local radio and television stations
- Local cable systems
- State and regional radio networks
- Television networks
- Cable networks
- Station representative companies (firms in big cities that represent local stations to national advertisers)

Places You'll Go

Beginners and experienced salespeople: Little potential for travel

Out-of-town travel is generally limited to regional or national sales or broadcast conventions or training seminars.

ENTERTAINMENT

Surroundings

Generally speaking, broadcast stations and cable systems are clean and comfortable places to work. However, for much or most of their day, sales reps are out calling on clients, whose work environment may vary from an upscale clothing boutique to a car repair shop. Today many reps save time by using a cellular phone to keep in touch with the office or to make calls while in transit.

Dollars and Cents

According to the National Association of Broadcasters, commercial TV salespeople's salaries averaged $48,671 overall in 1992. Sales reps in the top ten network-affiliate TV markets (stations affiliated with NBC, ABC, CBS or Fox) averaged $86,676; in the smallest affiliate markets they averaged $35,182. Salespeople at the top ten independent TV markets averaged $83,942; at the smallest, $38,073.

Radio sales reps overall averaged $37,690 in 1993, according to the annual salary survey for the industry publication *Radio & Records*. Reps in the 15 largest markets averaged $51,203; below the top 100 markets they averaged $27,864. The highest-paid reps often earn twice as much.

Moving Up

Ambition and drive go a long way; being a consistent sales producer is the single most important factor in success. The sales department is traditionally the most popular route to management. Typically, a successful sales rep moves up to assistant sales manager, then local or national sales manager and then general sales manager. Some reps keep selling but move up to bigger stations and bigger markets or deal with larger advertisers and national ad agencies. Other reps move into the creative departments of programming or news, join advertising agencies or go into market research.

Where the Jobs Are

Jobs are everywhere: There are nearly 10,000 commercial AM or FM radio stations and more than 1,150 commercial TV stations. Most sales jobs in cable are at the system level, and there are now more than 11,000 cable systems in the U.S.

◆ **Training**

Time salespeople generally learn the job on the job. It is difficult to train for this work in a classroom, though knowledge of sales and marketing theory is helpful. Internships (offered by some stations) are a great way to get on-the-job experience.

◆ **The Male/Female Equation**

Women now make up just over half of all salespeople in radio and broadcast television, and they are also well represented in cable sales.

◆ **Making Your Decision: What to Consider**

The Bad News
- Rejection comes with the job
- Clients can be demanding and difficult to please
- Hectic pace; constant pressure to "produce"
- Unpredictable pay, depending on commissions

The Good News
- Earning potential is very high
- Exciting and often glamorous field
- Constant opportunity to meet new and interesting people
- You're usually too busy to ever be bored

ENTERTAINMENT

What It's Really Like

Jim Skwiat, 26,
sales representative,
WGTC-FM/AM,
South Bend, Indiana
Years in the field: one

How did you get into radio sales?
I knew someone in the business who said it was a lot of fun. I loved this station—which plays country music—so I dropped off my resume and bugged the sales manager until I got the job.

What training or preparation did you have?
I joined the Marine Corps right out of high school and was trained as an engineer. While I was on active duty, I got my associate degree. While in the Reserves, I worked as a salesperson at a sporting goods store. Then I sold new cars for about a year and a half before moving into sales with a pharmaceutical packaging company. But my fiancée (now wife) hated my spending four and five days on the road, so I briefly joined another car dealership before I came here. All that experience was helpful—learning how to close a sale and selling door-to-door.

What was the hardest part of radio sales at the start?
Learning the numbers. Figuring up cost per (rating) point,

how much punch (the client gets) for the dollar, going into the Arbitron database to compare different stations in our market, where we fall, what our reach is, then putting together charts and bar graphs for presentations.

We have five salespeople here, plus the manager. I'm the only male. We don't have geographical territories; getting clients is strictly first come, first served. Our account list is updated constantly. Before you call on a business, you check to see if someone already has them.

What's a typical day like for you?
I come in around 7:30 A.M. and try to leave each day by 5 or 5:30 P.M. We have sales meetings three times a week. Mondays we learn about what's happening in the business and at the station. Wednesdays we do role-playing, such as how to present a new ad package. Fridays we brainstorm.

I go into the computer and pull numbers; I set up appointments with clients; I go out on calls. If I've targeted a new place, I'll go in and ask who makes the ad decisions, then make an appointment. My usual workweek is at least 50 hours. On weekends I go through my account list and figure out who I'm going to target next week.

How do you make a commercial sale?
At the initial interview with a prospect I'll ask a thousand questions. I get a feel for their business, who they're trying to target. Then I'll come back to the station and put together an order for the production department that lists all these points, and I'll say, "Make me a commercial that will hit females 25 to 35 who need a new car and want something sporty," and so on. Then I'll make another appointment with the prospect and play the tape—when they hear their name, it's a good way to close the sale. A lot of salespeople won't do all that; that's why it works for me.

My goal is to sign a client to a year's bulk contract, for 1,000 or 500 or 250 commercials.

What do you like most about your job?
When clients make money (from my ad program), I've helped them. A special promotion helps the client's customers, too, so it's win-win. Also, this is kind of a glamorous business. The day we announced we were bringing

ENTERTAINMENT

Garth Brooks to South Bend, friends called me for tickets.

What do you like least?
Pushing paperwork for all the orders and follow-up.

What advice would you give someone considering this field?
You need guts and patience. If you're scared to speak in front of people, don't get into radio sales. You have situations where you're talking to four or five people at the same time. I believe what (sales expert) Zig Ziglar says: Sales can be the hardest, best-paying job you ever had or the easiest, worst-paying job you ever had.

Sharon Miller, 35, account executive, Cable AdNet, Hurst, Texas
Time in the field: six months

What is your current position?
I sell commercial advertising on cable networks such as CNN, USA, ESPN, Lifetime and Discovery. We don't sell pay cable networks like HBO. Cable Ad Net represents four cable systems in the Dallas–Fort Worth metroplex.

How did you get into cable ad sales?
I'd been in sales in newspapers and direct mail for more than eight years. I was bored and complacent, and in sales that's a bad place to be. A former print colleague had come to Cable AdNet, and he pushed me to see the sales manager here. I told the manager I'd like to give cable sales a shot if she thought I had something to offer. I got the job, and I love it.

What was hardest about the job at the start?
Learning all about the 12 cable networks I sell so I could explain them with some credibility to clients. There's just so much to learn—who watches and when, the audience income and the male/female ratio. I also read all I could and went with the other salespeople on calls. I asked a lot of questions. I'm still learning.

TIME SALESPERSON

Is there a difference between selling print and electronic media?
Only in the product; sales is sales is sales. You still have to make a presentation, and you still need what we call BLT—believability, likableness and trust.

Broadcast (TV) and radio provide "reach," meaning they hit masses of people of various socioeconomic levels. Cable networks are skewed to specific demographic and geographic groups, so I can narrow the market down to the very specific clientele an advertiser is looking for. Also, because cable advertising is new to people here, they think it's expensive like broadcast and are surprised it's not. I can sell a 30-second spot for anywhere from $12 to $900.

How do you go about making a sale?
When you sell against other media, you don't badmouth them. I sold to some of my current clients when I was selling print, but I don't go in now and say, "Stop what you're doing." I ask, "What would you change about what you're doing? If this is working for you, let me show how it can work together with cable."

I take time to learn about their business; I try to watch out for their costs. My goal is to have my clients forever, so when they sign an agreement, they're stuck with me till death do us part. That's how you build a base.

What do you like most about this work?
The freedom to come and go. As a working mom, I'm able to be flexible. If I have to stay home with a sick child, I can still make phone calls and still make money. It's not an eight-to-five job; I put in the hours it takes to complete what I have to do. I've met clients at 6 A.M. if that's the only time I can catch them to go over their schedule, and I've gone to production with clients until midnight or 1 A.M. to be sure they're comfortable with the commercial. Sometimes I take clients to a sports event or go to an advertiser's grand opening. When I've had several nights like that, I might take a day off the next week.

What's the down side of the job?
We are not a known medium. Cable is still in its infancy as far as being considered a viable advertising alternative to broadcast. Also, cable has gotten a bad rap, especially

ENTERTAINMENT

about the cable regulation changes that irritated many subscribers in 1993. So we have to do a lot of educating.

What advice do you have for those interested in cable ad sales?
If you have no sales experience whatever, start from scratch somewhere. Start as an intern or a sales assistant or an administrative secretary and see how everything works.

Heidi Carmel, 29,
account executive, KVBC-TV,
Las Vegas, Nevada
Years in the field: three

How did you break into this business?
I was studying broadcasting at a community college, and I became an intern at radio station KOMP in 1987. During my three years there, I was public service director, production director and an on-air traffic and news personality. Then I decided to get into sales. I didn't want to sell for KOMP because it was an album-oriented rock station, and I didn't want to be in bars at night calling on clients. So I applied at an adult contemporary (soft hits) station, and they gave me a shot. I sold there for one year, then started interviewing here at Channel 3. Over a two-month period I interviewed with three people three times before I got hired.

Why did you want to switch from radio to TV sales?
Las Vegas is saturated with radio stations, over 40. I was having a hard time, and I started to think, Well, there's only one NBC television affiliate . . . plus the money is better.

What was the hardest part of the job at first?
It seemed like I was always stuck in the office doing paperwork; television probably has double the paperwork of radio. It also was hard learning about the different programs and who they're targeting; each program has a different demographic. By contrast, a radio station usually has one music format and one main group of listeners.

TIME SALESPERSON

Paperwork aside, I've found TV is an easier sell. We carry a videocassette player with us on sales calls so we can show examples of commercials we've done. We try to be well-rounded in marketing; I always tell my clients to support their TV ad schedule with radio.

What's a typical day like on the job?
I'm in the office by eight, and I do paperwork. Businesses don't open till 9 or 10 A.M. I set up appointments and try to go out on calls during the day and take clients to lunch. Usually we all come back at the end of the day to check in. A typical workweek is 50 to 60 hours. I have 50 clients, and I try to see everyone or at least make phone contact as often as possible. Occasionally I'll meet a client for dinner.

We initially ask prospective clients a lot of questions: Is your customer a blue-collar man? Is he a businessman who carries a cellular phone? How much is your average sale? Who do you specifically want to target? Then we use psychographic marketing studies to do a profile of the customer the client wants and put together a proposal for an ad program based on all that.

Are you involved in the production of commercials?
Yes. The ad copywriter will come on the call with me to get copy points from the client. Then, with my input, the copywriter does a script, and I take it to the client for approval. I also go on the shoot if I can.

What do you like most about this work?
Helping to make a client successful. I like to hear that business is booming and that they attribute it to their advertising.

What do you like least?
Clients who are disrespectful of my time—missing appointments or treating me like I need them more than they need me. I've had male clients who think I don't know what I'm doing. They make comments like, "Send your boss, honey, and then we'll talk." I tell them that I'm quite capable of making ad decisions and I don't need to send my boss—who also happens to be a woman.

ENTERTAINMENT

MORE INFORMATION PLEASE

Actor/Actress

The major trade publications include *The Hollywood Reporter, Backstage, Variety* (daily and weekly) and *American Theatre.*

Film and theater bookshops publish everything from plays and film scripts to guidebooks on agents and acting teachers. For catalog information, contact Samuel French, Inc., 45 West 25th St., New York, New York 10010 (800-8-ACT-NOW; in California: 800-7-ACT NOW). Acting publications also are available from the Drama Bookshop, 723 Seventh Avenue, New York, New York 10019 (800-322-0595).

Disc Jockey

The annual *Broadcasting & Cable Yearbook* lists all U.S. radio stations and their location, market position, power, programming format and management personnel.

Stagehand

Many of IATSE's 800 autonomous union locals have an apprentice program. Contact the local in your region or write the national office: IATSE, 1515 Broadway, Suite 601, New York, New York 10036-5741.

Theater production apprenticeships and internships are listed in the "Career Development" section of *ArtSEARCH*, a biweekly employment newsletter for the performing arts. For subscription information, contact *ArtSEARCH*, Theatre Communications Group, 355 Lexington Avenue, New York, New York 10017-0217 (212-697-5230).

Helpful trade publications include *Theatre Crafts* and *American Theatre* magazines and *Backstage,* the weekly newspaper.

MORE INFORMATION PLEASE

Cameraperson

Helpful industry publications include *American Cinematographer, Film and Video, The Hollywood Reporter*, weekly *Variety* and *Premiere*.

Time Salesperson

Industry publications include *Advertising Age, Broadcasting & Cable, Multichannel News, Cablevision Magazine, Radio & Records, Cable World, Electronic Media* and *Variety*.

Information and article reprints about radio sales careers are available from the Radio Advertising Bureau, 304 Park Avenue South, New York, New York 10010.

General

Extensive lists of sponsors of workshops and seminars in film and video, training programs and specialty schools in broadcast production, companies and organizations that offer intern programs in various television-related areas (including sales and marketing) and a bibliography of helpful books and pamphlets are included in *Career Opportunities in Television, Cable, and Video* by Maxine K. and Robert M. Reed (third edition, 1990, Facts on File). The book can usually be found in large libraries.

The free booklet *Women on the Job: Careers in the Electronic Media* is available from American Women in Radio and Television, 1101 Connnecticut Avenue, NW, Suite 700, Washington, D.C. 20036.

Careers in Radio and *Careers in Television* can be ordered for $3 each from the National Association of Broadcasters. For information, call NAB Services at 800-368-5644.

The booklet *Careers in Cable*, which offers an overview of all opportunities in the cable industry, can be ordered for $5 from the National Cable Television Association, Industry Communications Department, 1724 Massachusetts Avenue, NW, Washington, D.C. 20036.

ENTERTAINMENT

WILL YOU FIT INTO THE ENTERTAINMENT WORLD?

Before you sign up for a program of study or start to look for one of the jobs described in this book, it's smart to figure out whether that career will be a good fit given your background, skills and personality. There are several ways to do that, including:

❏ Talk to people who already work in that field. Find out what they like and don't like about their jobs, what kinds of people their employers hire, and what their recommendations are about training. Ask them if there are any books or publications that would be helpful for you to read. Maybe you could even "shadow" the workers for a day as they go about their duties.

❏ Use a computer to help you identify career options. Some of the most widely used software programs are *Discover*, by the American College Testing Service; *SIGI Plus*, developed by the Educational Testing Service; and *Careers*, by Peterson's. Some public libraries make this career software available to library users at little or no cost. The career counseling or guidance office of your high school or local community college is another possibility.

❏ Take a vocational interest test. The most common are the Strong Interest Inventory and the Kuder Occupational Interest Survey. High schools and colleges usually offer free testing to students and alumni at their guidance and career planning offices. Many career counselors in private practice or at community job centers can also give the test and interpret the results.

❏ Talk to a career counselor. You can find one by asking friends and colleagues if they know of any good ones. Or contact the career information office of the adult education division of a local college. Its staff and workshop leaders often do one-on-one counseling. The job information services division of major libraries sometimes offer low- or no-cost counseling by appointment. Or check the yellow pages under the heading "Vocational Guidance."

But first, before you spend time, energy or money doing any of the above, take one or more of the following five quizzes (one for each career discussed in the book). The results can help you evaluate whether you have the basic traits and abilities that are important to success in that career.

If you dream of a career as an actor on stage or screen, take this quiz:

Read each statement below, then choose the number 0, 5 or 10. The rating scale below explains what each number means.

>**0** = Disagree
>**5** = Agree somewhat
>**10** = Strongly agree

___I'm a disciplined and highly motivated person
___I don't mind speaking in front of a lot of people; I'm a bit of a ham
___I'm able to memorize lines of dialogue easily
___I can handle criticism pretty well; I listen and try to learn from it

ENTERTAINMENT

___I don't take rejection personally
___I'm very reliable; people know they can count on me
___I love the excitement of the theater and think I'd enjoy being a performer
___I have a lot of self-confidence
___I am able to take direction in my work
___I've been told that I have talent as an actor, singer or dancer

Now add up your score. ___Total points

If your total points are less than 50, you probably don't have sufficient interest in acting or the inclination to learn what's required. If your total points are between 50 and 75, you may have what it takes to get into the field, but be sure to do more investigation by following the suggestions at the beginning of this section. If your total points are 75 or more, it's highly likely that you are a good candidate for an acting career.

If you envision a career talking and playing music as a disc jockey, take this quiz:

Read each statement below, then choose the number 0, 5 or 10. The rating scale below explains what each number means.

0 = Disagree
5 = Agree somewhat
10 = Strongly agree

___I'm very reliable and punctual, and I have a strong work ethic
___I love music and have some musical knowledge
___I speak well and can clearly convey information
___It doesn't fluster me to keep track of more than one thing at a time
___I am detail-oriented and organized
___I've been told that I have a "terrific" voice
___I wouldn't mind working in one place all day
___I work well by myself

WILL YOU FIT IN?

___I know how to pronounce and use words correctly
___I can think on my feet and improvise when necessary

Now add up your score. ___Total points

If your total points are less than 50, you probably do not have sufficient interest in becoming a disc jockey or the inclination to learn what's required. If your total points are between 50 and 75, you may have what it takes to get into the field, but be sure to do more investigation by following the suggestions at the beginning of this section. If your total points are 75 or more, it's highly likely that you are a good candidate for this career.

If you're interested in a career as one of the behind-the-scenes stagehands who helps shine the spotlight on others, take this quiz:

___I usually stay calm under time pressure
___I'm willing to work long and unpredictable hours
___I'm the dependable type; people know they can count on me
___I can concentrate on getting my work done amid "organized chaos"
___I like to see immediate results for my efforts
___I like being part of a team, working toward a common goal
___I'm the physical type; I have a lot of stamina and strength
___I'm adept with basic tools and equipment or would be interested in learning how to use them
___I don't mind staying behind the scenes, helping others to look good
___I like the idea of not working in an office in a nine-to-five job

Now add up your score. ___Total points

If your total points are less than 50, you probably do not have sufficient interest in being a stagehand or the inclination to learn what's required. If your total points are between 50 and 75, you may have what it takes to get into

ENTERTAINMENT

the field, but be sure to do more investigation first by following the suggestions at the beginning of this section. If your total points are 75 or more, it's highly likely that you are a good candidate for a career behind the scenes.

If the idea of being a camera operator and looking through a lens for a living appeals to you, take this quiz:

Read each statement below, then choose the number 0, 5 or 10. The rating scale below explains what each number means.

> **0** = Disagree
> **5** = Agree somewhat
> **10** = Strongly agree

___I am healthy and in good physical shape, with no back problems
___I love the idea of working in video or film production
___I like being part of a team, working toward a common goal
___I am good at problem-solving
___I don't mind taking direction from others
___I'm always interested in learning new ways of doing things, being "state-of-the-art"
___I love photography; I like to experiment with cameras or video equipment for different effects
___I'm not bothered by long hours or hard work
___I'm comfortable with technical subjects and the sciences
___I'm an organized, methodical type of person

Now add up your score. ___Total points

If your total points are less than 50, you probably do not have sufficient interest in being a camera operator or the inclination to learn what's required. If your total points are between 50 and 75, you may have what it takes to get into the field, but be sure to do more investigation first by following the suggestions at the beginning of this section. If your total points are 75 or more, it's highly likely that you are a good candidate for this career.

WILL YOU FIT IN?

If you're a self-confident "people person" interested in a career as a time salesperson, take this quiz:

Read each statement below, then choose the number 0, 5 or 10. The rating scale below explains what each number means.

0 = Disagree
5 = Agree somewhat
10 = Strongly agree

___ I have a lot of determination and don't give up easily
___ I don't take rejection personally
___ I'm very outgoing and can talk easily with people I've just met
___ The idea of asking people to buy something from me doesn't make me uncomfortable
___ I'm comfortable with numbers and computers
___ I'm the type who always asks people a lot of questions, and I listen to the answers
___ I often make lists or notes of things I have to do
___ I like the idea of a workday that has routine yet is very flexible
___ I can keep my cool and remain productive under pressure
___ I like the challenge of identifying a problem and figuring out its solution

Now add up your score. ___ Total points

If your total points are less than 50, you probably do not have sufficient interest in becoming a salesperson or the inclination to learn what's required. If your total points are between 50 and 75, you may have what it takes to get into the field, but be sure to do more investigation first by following the suggestions at the beginning of this section. If your total points are 75 or more, it's highly likely that you are a good candidate for time sales.

ABOUT THE AUTHOR

Freelance writer and editor Linda Peterson lives in the New York City area. Formerly a staff editor at *Glamour* and *Ladies' Home Journal,* she also has written or edited for *Redbook, Working Woman, McCall's, Longevity* and *First for Women.* She is a columnist and contributing editor for *Arts & Entertainment Monthly.* This is the second *Careers without College* book she has written. The first, *Emergencies,* was published in 1993.

LEE COUNTY LIBRARY SYSTEM
3 3262 00177 2059
DISCARD

6/98

791
P
Peterson
Careers without college:
    Entertainment

LEE COUNTY LIBRARY
107 Hawkins Ave.
Sanford, NC 27330

GAYLORD S